PRIDE AND PREJUDICE: NAVIGATING LGBT IDENTITY IN INDIA

DAN

Contents

I

Introduction

My Name is Dan, that is not my actual name but it is a pseudo name I got from the internet. It was quite a neutral name and I probably had a good feeling about it so I went with this pen name.

Since many writers write under false names or like to call them by their pen names I felt to do the same thing as the topic I am writing about is very controversial and people around me are unaware of my identity. Neither my family nor my friends are aware of my sexuality, I have been a closeted bisexual for a very long time and I think it will take some time for me to come out of the closet.

I am sure there are a lot of nonfiction books on LGBT topics and in my book, I try to mix my own experience along with well-documented things or news that are already reported to make my case and maybe some folks might be able to relate with me.

I will not be providing the solutions, I am sure most of the stuff you might have heard or might be knowing which again begs the question why on earth am I writing this book? There is a powerful purpose for which I am writing this book.

An incident happened that changed my perspective on this current scenario and I was being targeted for my sexuality. It didn't happen to me in real life but on social media, I was on a platform called X formerly known as Twitter and I was using an alias username.

I made a mistake and people there eventually found out about my sexuality many people pushed me on the platform. Suddenly I was trying to defend myself and the thing that I had represented and for the first time, I felt that I should defend my honour and they could not get away with this.

One thing led to another and eventually, there was an army of such accounts I don't know if they work on someone's payroll or if they like to bully just to boost their ego, and before I could realize my comment section was filled with hateful things and they were so many that I just lost track all of that.

Eventually, the cyberbullying was so much that my every tweet would be met with some or other nasty things and DM would be filled with all such things spending time on social media became a curse for me as I felt hopeless and finally gave up and had to delete my Twitter account.

My mental health had been damaged due to that incident, I never thought that I would have been targeted like this because such an incident had never happened before in my lifetime even though I had heard about online harassment now I know what targeted harassment feels like and I went offline and it took me a while to recover and I realised something significant.

This happened online on a social media platform and I ran away because you can run away if things get too much but what if this had happened in real life? I cannot run away like that in real life as I have a family, a home. What would I do when this hits me in the worst possible way if they were to know about my sexuality?

Now some would argue that I am freaking out without any reason but as someone who has never faced this situation, I would say that I am right in my assumption even though this might seem like I am paranoid which I don't think I am.

India is not some Western country, people here care for morality and you will have wolves in sheep's clothing wanting to exploit you and suck you away for their good. Yes obviously I will not be killed just for being bisexual but there are plenty of other consequences that we might have to face due to this.

Homosexuals are treated in a way that it is some kind of mental illness for them and they have to be cured. There is a stigma against those whether they are homosexual or bisexual or even any other sexual orientation who are not straight.

Some families might be so strict that they would have a hard time accepting that their kid might not be the same way that they might have perceived him to be. Some families do accept although they are quite confused regarding the concepts and end up having some other picture of that certain fact.

In the past, we have seen a lot of news where people from the LGBT community were harassed, online or offline, and some of them were murdered mostly by someone from their own family.

There are hundreds of cases where people from the LGBT community have committed suicide or were killed which is tragic because your sexual preference can ignite such a radical response from those people around you.

And if you are not dead and still alive, you are looked down on as some alien species and there is a fear of judgment it will also eat you that someone at some other point in time would try to tell you that you are wrong and you need to change yourself.

Anyway coming back to my story I never came out of my closet due to all the factors mentioned and I have seen so many folks who have admitted but then again I never did and I don't think I ever will.

I don't want unnecessary drama in my life. I don't have the patience to tackle those humans and I have other things in my life and I just can't risk it with my current scenario.

My life is already sensitive, and I don't want to mess it up. I have always been reserved so I think it makes sense to never let it out. At this point, it may be surprising why I am writing this and what exactly the need for it.

The incident which happened on Twitter made me realise even though I am not ready to come out due to various reasons, I just want to write my heart out without getting bullied and writing this book can be a great source of happiness for me.

It also made me think that maybe there are others, people who don't know me or have never met me might read this and find my experiences to be similar to those in their lives as well. Although things are slowly changing in this country, we as a society still think it will take a long time for us to be accepted like normal folks.

Now one would argue that there are a lot of changes happening and Section 377 was decriminalised I think it was a great step in accepting us and legally we still have a long way to go and I am not going to discuss the legality or history of our community but rather culturally where we stand and our future and our experiences whether good or bad both have shaped us to be in this position.

Films have often played a major role in our society and can influence many minds, especially the younger generation. Most of the mainstream Indian movies which I have watched display homosexuals and transgenders in a very negative light.

Some of the scenes are very offensive and can be termed as racist and homophobic and even call for violence against those who behave in such a way. Men are supposed to behave in a certain way and if they don't then that means they might be gay person.

In those movies, effeminate men are often perceived as gay and are generally portrayed as weaker men who are impotent. Major film studios have set these narratives, adding fuel to the existing fire.

I am not blaming movies for the current scenario but they have played a major role in that narrative like they legitimised the hate against homosexuals and transgenders. Most folks barely know the reality of homosexuals and transgenders and I don't expect them to know anything about bisexuals.

Well-known celebrities who have come out as gay, people still considered weirdos who need mental treatment. In my personal life, I have seen people who have used strong language against homosexuals in general and sometimes I do feel attacked but then I just try to avoid those people as much as I can.

I sometimes wonder what would happen if they knew I was a bisexual. I mean the number of questions they would ask and my answers would never satisfy them. I don't know how their behaviour would be around me, would they be feeling disgusted by me, surprised by me?

I was never interested in pride parades but now I get the significance and I am even curious to join any pride parade near me. It is interesting to see several pride parades increasing every year, I guess folks will feel compelled to join this parade sooner or later or eventually come out.

Culturally India has not been opposed to people of different sexuality, there have been stories of queer people in the past and present, so it is interesting where this mentality of hating queers, in general, comes from.

In recent times we have had a big athlete who happens to be a sprinter come out as lesbian, I did not witness any in India from sports coming out so yeah I think it is great that more and more people are coming out.

Similarly, we have a big-time film producer who is well-known and has admitted to being gay but then again these are exceptions I guess. Yes, things are better compared to a previous couple of decades but I still feel there is a lot of stigma around this.

I am not a fan of classification but I am afraid I will have to classify households, one who hails from a conservative background and another who hails from a progressive background.

Let's talk first about how a lot of folks feel that it is easy when you are from a progressive background, well I come from a very progressive background and sometimes I find it amusing how they can accept one and another thing.

Despite coming from a progressive and upper middle class, my situation is like this where I have to wonder if I won't be judged or perceived in a bad way and being judged and perceived is from one dimension, I am more afraid regarding repercussions.

I hate being around those people who feel pity on me or who feel like I am an alien and I think my situation would fit either one of these, after all, I should consider myself lucky that I was born into such a good family.

Now I am sure that this kind of situation is not limited to me several folks might be able to relate to that and explaining it to them is very difficult. They have a tough time accepting homosexuality and eventually, they come back to the original question.

I think explaining my sexuality to my loved ones is even more complicated than my job profile. When I got a job, many folks were curious about what my job was and what I did. Well, I tried my best to let them know what a content writer was and its job description.

Every time I tried to tell time what I did for a living, I failed miserably and that was me trying to explain my sexuality to them. They would go bonkers and my social life would get so awkward which is already so awkward.

That day I realised that I could not explain my job description when I was employed and would have so many questions which I didn't have the patience maybe it was better for everyone that I didn't disclose this piece of information.

Coming back to folks who come from conservative backgrounds well they are doomed. When they even think about it, they feel like it is just a temporary thing, phase or some ill-minded thought which will be eventually cured by heterosexuality.

They think that with time and as they grow up they will not face such a dilemma after all that is what has been taught to them since childhood that homosexuality or queerness is a disease, if you have it then it is a huge problem.

Some folks convince themselves that they are indeed heterosexual while others are not able to do so and eventually, when their family finds out there is so much drama that you will have to convince them there is nothing wrong which is the basic argument.

It doesn't matter if someone is homosexual, heterosexual, bisexual or not interested in sex at all. After all, these are personal choices to be made by that certain individual and not collectively by any organisation or society.

Now gays have a different set of problems and lesbians face altogether different kinds of problems, especially in a country like India where you have to get married at a certain age and you need to maintain some beauty standards and other things you have to survive as a woman.

Just like being gay or bisexual is not easy and one has to face a lot of challenges, being a lesbian has its struggles. Generally, if such information is leaked to the family, they first want to get her married.

Probably that is the universal solution offered nowadays every time they have to reject the idea their kid or someone they know has to get married and all these thoughts they are getting due to loneliness.

Some do get married and the results of those marriages could be devastating, it could potentially destroy 2 families not to mention the number of people it has destroyed and in case someone does anything which might be termed inappropriate it eventually destroys a lot of people so yeah marriage is not the solution.

Marriage between 2 individuals is a very complex thing, a lot of parents in a hurry do something which can have an everlasting effect. Imagine the scenario of a homosexual getting married to a heterosexual, their partner would have thought of so many wonderful moments with them and instead, their heart gets broken.

Eventually, everyone will get to know the truth and there will be a lot of feud between the couple and their families. It is hard to say what the future of the couple, would be even if they are counselled to continue marriage it would be horrible and if they decide to part ways there will always be the feeling of betrayal.

Sure you can argue that it is best to part ways, being in such a marriage could have a lasting impact on mental health and we do not know how both people involved in this relationship would do shortly. Many possibilities could happen both positive and negative.

II

My Experience as Bisexual

It is hard to say when I discovered my sexuality, my classmates in school would often think that I was gay because I did not have a girlfriend at that time and I find this behaviour amusing because not having a girlfriend can make people assume stuff.

At that point, I could not answer them because I already had an intimate experience with a boy and I was quite passionate about him but with time we realized that our relationship at any cost could not become known to the public.

Having a girlfriend at that age would be considered controversial and if someone knew about my boyfriend, all hell might have broken loose, I was still in school so I didn't know the consequences of such actions.

I don't know much about love but he was my first love, we had some great moments together and some intimate moments spent together were some of the best of my life.

But then again reality hit hard, and we realised that the relationship could not continue, he was not comfortable putting his and my life at risk. He was particularly worried about me and I respected his decision and we haven't talked in a while.

Coming back to my school, I didn't know one generation back that there was this much pressure to be in a relationship. From the stories I heard back as a kid, they were quite innocent and would not have any information regarding this subject and the newer generation is very fast compared to the previous.

Most of the folks whom I have met from previous generations are quite homophobic, I have not personally experienced this because I never told them about my sexuality but some of the comments which I cannot tell here have been very racist.

Every time I meet them they somehow manage to ask me about my marriage and I try my best to dodge that question but I think there will come a time when I will no longer be able to dodge that question and my secret will eventually be out.

It is interesting to see how that part of my life would play out. I don't hate the concept of marriage, marriage could be a good thing after all if we look at it from a philosophical point of view then it is supposed to be a bond between 2 people who try to create good memories for themselves.

Furthermore, they make babies and therefore the general assumption is that the couple along with the babies should make a wholesome family which would take care of each other when in need but then again in theory this sounds great in reality things could be a lot different.

Even if I get a partner to get married to someone I would like a full disclosure if they accept for what I am then there is a chance that marriage could work otherwise it is doomed even before it begins.

If I were to disclose my sexual identity, I think there would be very few takers and not to mention the kind of homophobia I encounter online from time to time only gives me confidence that in the real world, it would be far worse.

Yes, we talk about being progressive and accepting but I am afraid that is just lip service, just like equality. Folks from all sections of the country talk about equality only on paper but the reality is different altogether.

Gender Equality is something a lot of women have been talking about and trying to implement for the last 2 decades but then again we see so much that is happening but to an ordinary individual it barely impacts them.

I am not against gender equality or anything that promotes equality, but I want to say that we may assume things to be happening in theory. Still, in reality, things are very different. We might think that we have come so far, but in reality, we might not.

Anyway after that breakup, I became cautious, I did not want anyone to notice my sexuality. I started monitoring my behaviour, I mean at one point in time I started to feel paranoid like a criminal who was afraid his crime would be exposed sooner or later.

Surely I was paranoid throughout the relationship but after the relationship, it was as if I had done something terrible. My anxiety and stress were at an all-time high and I was trying my best to act in a cool and calm way and not get carried away by the emotions.

Every time I would feel attracted to a man I would ensure to keep my eyes under control after all this would be a disaster and if someone from my family noticed I couldn't even imagine the kinds of questions I would be asked.

During my school days, I was already suffering with my average grades and I didn't want another problem at one point in time I had enough of those lectures I would get for random stuff.

Imagine what would happen if they were to find out this secret of mine and the amount of pressure and counselling they would do just because I like men it would be my worst nightmare and with no one to seek advice I was doomed at that stage of my life.

That was probably the worst phase of my life and I survived it somehow by that time I was convinced that pursuing another homosexual relationship would be a very dangerous thing so I went to the internet in the hope no one would find me.

And things were even more crazier on the internet, the kind of homophobia. Although there were some really good experiences on the internet, I met some new people online but there were some horrible experiences.

That incident which happened on Twitter was not the first time, I have been called faggot several times and initially, I did not know what it was but eventually found out the meaning and I would say that I was hurt emotionally.

Anyway, returning to my pleasant experiences, it was wonderful to know some people. I have known people of both genders and people from different countries, cultures and sexualities. I learned so much from them and it is good to see there is so much positivity in the world.

We often talk about how things are so bad that we face so much hate and abuse for our identity, it is nice to see there are pleasant things in the same world. Yeah, that doesn't still change the fact of the abuse and hatred that is being spread online.

I am surprised at the fact so many social media platforms claim to tackle bullying and hate speech, yet their actions are so different from their words. It is amusing to see some of the words that have been normalised.

Most of these platforms are run by people living in the West where you are supposed to feel space in their platforms and they claim to be inclusive and progressive, sounds like sugarcoating to me.

I mean I have come across posts on these social media where open death threats were given and the post was still there which makes you wonder if this is the scenario if it is run by progressives what if the conservatives were to run these platforms?

I mean I see folks on the right complain that all the major platforms, social media, google, YouTube and other stuff are heavily left-leaning platforms and yet we have a scenario where extreme violence against people of a certain sexuality is normalised and every day these things are common.

It is kind of absurd the amount of hate I see on the internet against homosexuals or bisexuals and the bullying goes as well. The story I told you at the start was just one of the several stories folks like me have experienced.

There have been people from the younger generation who either feel like dying or have killed themselves due to that pressure. It is not only disturbing and sad that now and then we hear stories but they are labelled as freaks and losers.

I think this is one of the major reasons people who do not live in the West have problems. On one side we talk about freedom and nothing is stopping anyone from doing whatever they feel like and on the other hand these incidents have time again proved that it is still not safe.

Even if something happens to a certain individual, no action will be taken against those individuals who have bullied and pressured him to do certain extreme steps. They may be fine with someone else's kid being homosexual but the moment the same thing hits your own home the behaviour changes completely.

I am saying this because this is a common argument that is used. We will not kill you, harm you or bully you but this comes with terms and conditions. I am talking in respect to my country and geographically it might be different for you.

They may call you all bad sorts of things and might either try to kill you or break your relationship. I don't know what is worse, living in a country where you could be executed or in a country where things get so messed up you might be just tired of this.

Anyway coming back to my country, it is fine as long as a person from another family comes out of the closet and they might just avoid him. But the moment this thing hits your home, things and behaviour become completely different.

There will be 2 kinds of behaviour you will usually notice from them, one would be very aggressive kind of behaviour which will stop at nothing until you give up to them and another behaviour is the softer approach where they would try to convince you in the best way possible.

One method is the direct approach and they are honest in their intentions whereas the other method they try to sugarcoat you with sweet words and try to change your sexuality by offering things.

They might tell you that you are like this because you are not married and that is why you are having such thoughts and you are not so different from other people. It is due to loneliness you are behaving in such a manner.

Some people who are already confused about their sexuality will be even more confused and some folks might start to think they should give it a chance and see what happens well if you take their advice you will end up disappointing yourself.

Every time there is a situation that must be solved or they are in a tricky situation, they recommend a marriage. Most of those folks are not wise and can barely understand the situation so they do what was taught to them since childhood.

They have one solution for all problems, they think that humans are rigid beings where theoretical solutions would match real-world situations and often these perfect solutions come with dangerous consequences.

Anyway, now that they are trying to convince you of a solution, you might have to accept their solution or reject it. If you accept their solution well you just complicate your entire life and if you don't accept their advice well the answer remains the same just the dimensions are changed.

Sadly, we have to defend the point that just like different people can have different opinions, people can have different sexualities and it is not some mental illness or disease. I mean if you are not straight then you don't have to be counselled.

It is not a mistake to be not a straight person, our habits are different, and our tastes are different so naturally the kind of people we are getting attracted to are also different. It might be hard for someone who has had not much exposure to different kinds of sexualities to understand.

They label everything under one umbrella term, oh since you are gay you must be like him, I didn't know lesbians could have feelings as well I thought it was just a phase. Oh, you are transgender so you are gay or what?

These are some of the assumptions which are randomly thrown at LGBT people and these are just nice examples some of them could be harsh with their words. Some folks get accepted although the population of such people is very low but still, they do exist.

I feel great whenever I imagine it in my mind or when I see it on the internet even though I do not know them, I still feel you should be cherished wherever you are and hopefully, you and your family are still close.

There was a Starbucks ad I think some time back that the family accepted their trans daughter and there were a lot of folks who didn't like the ad itself saying that Starbucks has gone completely woke.

Just one ad was able to produce such a reaction, I have read replies to that ad and it was pathetic to see so many comments against it some were calling it to boycott Starbucks, and others called this activism. There were some comments to keep this disease out of India.

The YouTube comment section was filled with such transphobia and I don't know if the transgender community in India is aware of such controversy personally it pains me, we may argue that we are making it a safe space for all individuals but the ground reality is different.

We may think that situation was so better for this community than it was let's say 10 or 20 years ago and here we have an ad, nothing controversial was said in the ad and yet it manages to get a polarizing reaction from such a huge number of people.

It is not that 5 or 10 comments are like that, I would say 90% of comment sections on Twitter and YouTube for this particular video generated similar responses to what I have been describing earlier that they feel like you are something different from them who needs to be either taught a lesson or be treated as some form of mental illness.

I see a lot of folks say that this reaction usually comes from men but not from women because women are empathetic beings and they can understand other people's pain. Unfortunately in my experience that is not the truth women can be as homophobic or transphobic as men.

Of late, I have been reading stories on Reddit, some of the folks happen to be in India and the stories are heartbreaking, if you are someone who is active on Reddit and follows lgbt subreddit then you would know what I am talking about.

Anyway I have tried multiple sites on the internet, looking to get connected with singles from other countries and the experience was mixed mostly, some experiences were good, and others could have been better.

I have been on Facebook and then on some virtual world sites and then have used these random chats like kik. On each of these platforms, my experience has been different and there have been some horrible experiences as well. I will try to differentiate how it is different for different sites.

Firstly I would like to start with Facebook, I think Facebook is a great place to get to know more about friends you have lost contact with. I wouldn't say that it is a great place for dating since there are specialized apps for such things but in those days Facebook was quite popular.

After Google Facebook was the most popular site even Reddit was not popular in my country. Now I haven't used it in years but back in the day, chatting was quite easy and in fact, I was surprised by the number of people I was in contact with even though I never met them or they probably never saw my face.

There was this woman I was in contact with, she didn't know English and I was using Google Translate to keep in touch with her. Then, it felt like some kind of achievement now I don't even feel proud of it as it has become common.

It was fun the casual flirting and playing games, there was this game called spin the bottle I think, you could get the possibility whether or not to give a kiss to the user and yeah it was a wild game even though it was through the internet it had caused so many controversies if I remember it well.

And since people would be uncomfortable sharing their mobile numbers they were fine with sharing their Facebook ID so it was kind of easy and then you were able to know what's happening in other countries as well.

Virtual world sites were wonderful and I didn't know what could be done there. I was looking for casual dating but with more anonymity and that is when I got to know about virtual world games or sites.

There are multiple virtual world games or sites, technically it is called a game because it is like a video game but then again you have an animated version of yourself exploring this world. Depending upon the type of site that is being used you can do different activities.

This was not your typical Facebook game where you play a multi-player game but this is like an alternate universe where you could be whatever you want to be. You can dress whichever you want, you can give a desired look, hairstyle and body yourself.

In one of them, you could fly in the air and explore the skies or go underwater to explore the sea life I would say the creators of this have done a wonderful job and you could make in-game coins which were something new for me.

You could meet people, talk with them and hang out with them just like you would do in real life, it felt like a real-life simulation where you could talk to people. I met some good people and some horrible people on this platform.

When I went to those sites it was like I had come into an alternate reality and I was able to dictate what I could be. Money was not the issue we have in real life and they are still popular today because of freedom.

When I say that it was almost like a simulated reality, you have to believe me it was indeed. For folks who are not aware of virtual world sites, it is like playing a multi-player video game where you would have to interact with people and the only difference is you just can't kill people here.

These sites are more settled versions of what humans dream of, you know a wonderful wife, kids, a house at the beach no tensions nothing just you having a good time with family. I feel that is the reason these became very popular with people of all ages.

Although this site seems like a dream, many things are happening that are different from what is considered morally accurate. A lot of folks who come on them are either committed or married in real life and yet they have a partner in the virtual world.

I read an article somewhere that a lot of marriages have been destroyed by these virtual games or sites whatever you want to call them. Because their real-life partner is unaware of the thing they are doing online and for them, it is not cheating.

But that is not true for their partner, they consider it to be cheating and just like video games these are addictive as well. You spent hours and hours being with that someone special ignoring your real life which could potentially destroy your relationship.

I was in love with a woman who was married in real life and I know this sounds crazy and very outrageous but that is a reality which I could not walk away from and neither could she. We had a great relationship and I knew very few things about her husband and kids sometimes we would talk about her real life but I realized it very late.

I had used predominantly these 3 sites namely Second Life, Smeet and IMVU and my experience has been pretty much the same though there exists some differences so far the story I was telling about this woman was from Second Life.

Although Second Life was not the virtual life I was using, there were several others. Second Life was probably the first game where I developed online friends and romantic relationships and I know this sounds crazy on so many levels.

I think very few people have heard about these games such as Second Life, some people have a very big problem with it while others have better apps for socializing and most of the social apps require you to post photos or at least that is what I thought when I signed up for these games and I thought I would be able to maintain my anonymity.

As a teenager or young adult, you like to explore things in your way. A lot of folks play multiplayer games, they have made friends and some do the same thing on Instagram or Facebook and I did the same thing in something called Second Life.

I have made a lot of friends so many friends on Second Life, I was kind of stunned because I always perceived myself as not good enough for socializing but here it is like I am a completely different person.

Did the game environment change me or is it because I have not been able to meet the right people? Perhaps there could be a third reason as well that maybe I might have social anxiety and when I am behind a mask I am confident since no one will judge me.

So coming back to the second life, I signed up for this game and I was able to select an avatar within a couple of minutes. I was transferred to this place, it was fascinating because the room I joined was a public room and this was that place where you could meet new people.

I was exploring that area and my character had a lot of options and I was able to swim, fly and run. There was this option of adding friends and the option of voice chat and yes you were able to message your friends which is quite common in most apps.

The rooms were fantastic and some rooms were frankly out of my imagination. There were garden rooms, there were cafe rooms and apartment rooms, islands, beaches, and popular cities such as Paris, Rome, LA City etc.

There were strip clubs where you would find these models and of course, she would do the dance thing for you if you paid her some money and you were able to have sex for a limited time.

My mind was frankly blown away by all this and I felt that I was in some kind of dream I had never been paid money for sex and I used some in-game money for cyber sex and yes there was guilt inside me.

I think I was facing a roller coaster of emotions when this happened to me and I think I happened to meet a woman I think she was much older than me and I was able to vent out she gave me a lot of guidance and she understood me probably more than I could understand myself.

Those days were wonderful, it was like a dream life and we would hang out daily. I think I failed to mention that in that game there were poses you know all you had to go and stand there and then depending on the pose you were able to kiss or have sex.

There were some of the dancing rooms where you could dance with your partner or do yoga. I think this was the place where I met her initially it was a simple conversation but eventually it led to more and more romantic talks and we became passionate about each other over time.

More than the dancing and sex, it was the intimate conversations which were close to my heart and I was addicted to her. I could not stop thinking about her things were going pretty well and then I got to know that she was married in real life.

It was the ultimate truth bomb, it sent shockwaves and it was like my entire relationship was flashing over my eyes ever since I met her. I didn't know what to say to her and for her, it was just a casual thing that slipped her mind and I was devastated inside.

Was this the norm of this game i mean was it some unwritten rule that whatever you do in this game stays in this game and you cannot complain about it if you want to mix game and real life eventually your heart would be broken because pretty much everyone has real life relationship and they are here for some time pass.

I kept avoiding that topic for a while and it was not as if she was bored by her real life, it was just that she wanted to have fun yes she did not say those exact words but that is the only conclusion I could make out of it.

Soon I realized that indeed pretty much everyone was like here and you would have been a fool if you were to invest emotions in such a game. For most, it is a game while there are others, it was not a game I had met a few of them and they had reciprocated similar feelings.

The more and more time I spent time with her the more I felt disconnected from reality. Eventually, I left Second Life and then went to another game called IMVU, I just left her a message that I would never see her. I don't know how she reacted hopefully she would forgive me and maybe then I could be at peace and just move on.

I was foolish enough to believe that only Second Life was like this and that other games were different and then I went to IMVU thinking that my experience would be different, boy I was disappointed again and IMVU was crazier than IMVU.

I had joined IMVU thinking that even though I didn't have much hope I wanted my experiences to be different and I met some good people, mostly my relationships were casual but then an unexpected event happened and my account was hacked.

It was horrible the hacker who did it sent vulgar messages from my profile to everyone who was on my friend list this created a huge misunderstanding they felt like I was some kind of a pervert who would send lewd messages.

I informed all my friends that my account had been hacked but by the time I had informed them that I was not responsible for it and someone else was responsible I thought it was too late and no one believed me and they all thought I was faking to get sympathy.

Out of all my friends, only 1 seemed to have trust in me with what I said we went out in a public room and that same hacker started writing messages on my behalf in a public room and this hacker said to me that he would not stop so eventually I had to delete my account.

It was a very brief period I had spent in IMVU, more than the relationships it was the hacking which had upset me the most. My experience was quite different in IMVU compared to Second Life although both the games were heartbreaking it was different heartbreaks and most of the relationships I had pursued were straight only.

One core difference between IMVU and Second Life was that IMVU was less of a real-life simulator and more of a chatting site as there are not many things to do whereas Second Life has so many activities and its world is high-speed.

Even if we were to compare the different types of rooms in both games, it was safe to say that Second Life was much better and it was much safer to use. My experience was that IMVU could have been more satisfactory.

I wanted to go back to the Second Life at that moment but I didn't dare to go back as I was afraid of what would happen if the woman whom I was in love with would somehow discover me, I could not take that risk.

Now that I think of my decision I don't consider it logical but still at that point I felt that I had made the right decision and I have no regrets. I was surfing for another game like this and then I stumbled on another game known as Smeet and it changed a lot of things in my life.

Smeet was different, I felt that there was more privacy compared to others and you could do a lot of activities and would not get bored due to the time difference every time I would log on there would be very few people and most of the rooms were empty and I was happy about it.

Compared to Second Life and IMVU, Smeet was better in times of my overall experience. Yes, you could argue that graphically it may be far behind and the no. of rooms it had was much less than the other 2 but still, there was a soothing experience.

Smeet had a lot of fun activities you could build your rooms and work on them, a feature which was never there in other games and most of the folks who were there were to do work rather than socialising.

Of Course, people would hang out and dance and chat and probably go on a date but there were very few rooms that had the environment in which you would be able to get an experience that you are there for a romantic evening.

I didn't hope that I would last this long on Smeet, I had used it for almost 4 years which was quite remarkable because I thought that I would not even last 6 months on this game since both my previous experiences have been not so good.

I liked the overall game style and the fact that you would be able to meet people and work was a pretty good combination. I think it is a combination of both professional and personal life in 1 game and eventually, I felt addicted to the game.

I would spend many hours playing this game and I didn't realise that I was wasting so many precious hours of mine. I was using it for about 6-8 hours daily and due to that, I was having irregular sleep schedules which had impacted my mental health.

I met some nice people on Smeet, a few of them from my own country and they shared their personal lives it was great chatting with them and getting to know them because in all these years I never knew that we would be sharing so much intimate information on a public platform.

I had become friends with a lot of folks and there was this girl who had changed my perspective on my life. I think we were passionate about each other, I asked her on a date and she readily agreed.

The mere idea of a date on a game sounded very foolish to me, after all, I never had asked someone in a game. Sure I was in many alleged online relationships but I had expressed my feelings directly to them instead of trying to know them.

It was a great date and we were coming close to each other emotionally and we were having a great time with each other and then she said something which complicated things forever, she said her ex came back into her life again and she was confused as she still has feelings for him.

This was again very devastating for me as I was starting to wonder if I was starting to develop a pattern here or maybe I should just stop dating women. Maybe I should see what men offer me and see where it takes me as I have given priority to women and it has given me disastrous results.

I was disinterested in meeting new people however as my perspective had changed suddenly and even if I were to meet someone there was a high probability that the final result would be the same as the previous ones.

I told myself that pursuing online relationships was probably one of the worst decisions of my life and instead, I need to focus on other things maybe friendship online is cool but nothing more than that and developing feelings is quite a stupid idea.

Casual Sexting is fine but to pretend that there is hope for a romantic relationship online is quite a waste of ideas and not worth pondering over. So I changed my entire approach and started to find guys and girls on the internet you know for just casual cybersex.

Initially, I was open to both genders but the main problem was that there were hardly any genuine women available on those sites. There were tons of catfish accounts and I don't know why on earth so many of the catfish accounts exist but they are pretty much everywhere.

One of the major reasons why there are so many catfish accounts online is the possibility that they never had that experience or they want to try out something and are afraid of getting judged.

You can easily find these apps or websites I guess where you randomly get matched to someone and then you can chat with them. There are 2 categories when it comes to chatting one is the video and the other is texting.

I don't have the guts to face the camera so I don't go to those sites which have an involvement with cameras as nowadays anyone can record anything and post online and you might go viral for no reason.

The last thing I want is anyone from my family enquiring about the shit I have been up to and yes if you have already read the previous stories I have been mentioning continuously then you should probably have an idea about what I am talking about.

So one thing was quite clear you would not be able to find any luck if you are heterosexual and looking for something there all you would get is men pretending to be women and if they send you pics then they are most likely to be lifted from google, you could try to reverse search image and you would get your proof.

You can find a lot of homosexuals and bisexuals in these chats just make sure that you don't leak much of the personal information as it may have bad consequences. Just try to keep casual and don't get carried with emotions, see if you can get connected on some other instant messaging so you can have prolonged fun.

As long as you have zero expectations nothing bad will happen and the moment you get attached or sentimental is where your problems start there is no solution for these kinds of problems.

Some of the men I had chatted with online were great men and I had a really fun time with them the only problem was that I didn't know how to contact them afterwards it was just a temporary 1-time fling and then the chances of getting reconnected were near to zero.

I don't recall many women on these kinds of sites mostly lesbians and I never talked to one of them because that was never my territory. Given the kind of creepy men that were there on this website, I would not expect a lot of women to be on these sites.

I mean normally on social media websites, they get harassed and cyberbullied and blackmailed so I could imagine the kind of behaviour that would happen on these so-called sex chat websites.

I mean yes it is easy sex technically it is not real sex but it still can give you pleasure some of the men I mean were disgusting and I encountered a few paedophiles and I felt disgusted and numb.

It took me a few days to come out of disbelief because I had heard about paedophiles only in movies and books but I had never met them either in real life or on the internet. To come face to face with not just 1 but several of them was something I had never expected.

At this point, I started to feel disgusted by myself and was starting to hate myself. I was having double thoughts about finding love on the internet or casual flings I was coming across. I started to feel like an immoral person who did not care for right and wrong.

Maybe I should pretend that I am a heterosexual just like the rest of the boys and try to find a suitable partner for myself just like all the other men who fall in my bracket age have done or are trying to do.

I don't know if that should have been a good plan and since I have lost touch with all my schoolmates and college mates I would have to start fresh if I was seeking a normal romantic relationship.

So the places where you meet your partner are school, college, work, party, getting introduced by family or friends and neighbours. I was pretty much disqualified from half of all those things mentioned.

I ignored all those girls interested in me in school and college. Yeah, I was an egoistic kind of person those days. Work was something which was a place where I could find a mate but then again you have to be very careful these days as it can have severe consequences.

No one invites me to parties and even if they do by chance I won't go to them and as far as getting introduced by family or friends are concerned I don't have interest in that as well which leaves the option of neighbours which is an interesting option for me.

This is not the first time I have noticed that a neighbour has shown interest in me and this has happened to me many times it is just I don't get the feeling that I should go for it. It might be seen as weird but every time I see a girl who is interested in me I just don't feel like dating her.

I don't know why it happens to me maybe I have not yet met that person who I would like to go all in for or maybe I am afraid of something of which I am not aware but at the end of the day, my love life has been quite weird even by my standards.

On some days I think I should try to become normal and do normal stuff just like the others are doing and on other days I feel like it is just not worth it and that I risk too much and a person of my sexuality should try to avoid these kinds of things.

I like to observe the so-called normal people in my life and they are fucked up in so many ways. It is interesting to know that I am not the only one living such a complicated life; in fact, some folks are probably living even worse than I could ever imagine.

I am glad that am not one of those who got married at a young age and now have to regret their whole life and blame things in life which will not give my life back or make my future worth living enough.

I have seen people in my life doing that and they always tell others to be careful when it comes to marriage as marriage is a very sacred thing and you should not do it as time passes. When I was a teenager I did not understand but as an adult, I was starting to understand what it means.

Workplace romances are a controversial topic and a lot of folks think that you should avoid them as they may cause a lot of legal troubles, if things go sour you never know what is going to happen to you.

If it turns up good then it is a blessing but if it turns out to be awful then you would have to see what you are up against and there is a chance you might lose your job or might face legal problems depending upon the action of the other person.

Now this may sound very judgemental of me but the reality is this is happening in the corporate sector and if you happen to work in say a big company then there is a lot of politics involved in this and we never know how things might turn out.

It is hard for me to get involved with any co-worker but then again I got involved with this woman who was much older than me and it was a temporary thing and it never evolved. Now the funny thing when I told this story to my friend she was worried.

She told me that I could get in trouble for doing that and I was surprised at her reaction and then I later realised that if the woman chooses to then she could file workplace harassment against these kinds of cases.

Despite the affair ending I think we were on good terms and probably that is the reason I was not expelled from my job ever since then I have been very cautious when it comes to workplace romance.

Anyway, I have left my job so I need not worry about that, in the past decade or so I have made some foolish things in my life and I won't be able to correct and there have been some of the mistakes which I have constantly been repeating so I do want to work on that.

I don't like change probably that is the reason my life is a hell lot of complicated than it was supposed to be at times I could be very judgemental and stubborn which I have tried to change but have been unsuccessful in doing so.

When I was in college I was a different person and by the time I quit my job I noticed some changes so surely we do change from time to time and it is the human tendency that after having different experiences your lifestyle might change and it may also change the way you are supposed to think.

Folks who are usually very carefree in their attitude, cannot have the same attitude they had in college, job, marriage, or responsibilities it changes the way you are. Maybe you cannot notice that but surely people around you will notice that and bring that to your notice.

However I would like to add despite these changes your overall personality remains the same, yes there would be some adjustments but you cannot change yourself completely. Some traits you would be able to change or alter but most of the stuff you want to change probably you won't be able to, I mean I have tried and failed miserably.

Just because I failed that doesn't mean that everyone does, my larger point is if you look at it from a psychological perspective then changing your personality is almost next to impossible although you can change a few aspects which everyone does in their life and maybe you might be feeling like a different person when you have altered some aspects of your life but the overall essence remains the same.

III

LGBT Rights in India

Although the LGBT Community is a very minority community still there is a lot of confusion regarding the different sexualities included in this community as there are a lot of different sexualities which have been identified with this community.

Although LGBT means that there are lesbian gay bisexual and transgender in recent times there have been people of different sexualities such as queer, and asexual have also been associated with it.

If we look at the past few decades then things have certainly improved I mean if we take a look at LGBT Rights in India. There has been a lot of advocacy and activism going on, especially in the urban areas.

Not everyone in the urban areas is LGBT friendly, I mean sure there might be some people who might be pro-LGBT but mostly I see the anti-LGBT sentiment. It is embedded right from childhood.

When I was a little and we used to go to our grandmother's house, we were taught about the special community who are not considered normal they are referred to as hijras and we were taught to stay away from them.

Well, years later I understood that being Hijra is quite different from being gay, both are not the same and there are a lot of differences but I didn't know back then. I used to put them all in the same bracket.

I wasn't even aware there were so many different sexualities growing up as I had very limited knowledge of what things are and I was ignorant at so many levels. I feel like I am not the only one who used to think like me there are many people like me.

I didn't know that whom I hated so much as a child I would be identifying one day and I never considered I would start identifying with the identity which I had hated as a kid. Amazingly, I have changed so much in these years.

LGBT Community in India rarely has any rights and to date, it doesn't have many rights but certain things are changing, it is no longer criminal to be a person of that community and I think it was a welcome move in the right direction.

There are still a lot of things that can be done to safeguard them, I think more than legally as the society they have to be embraced then only a proper change be brought. If we still think that it is unnatural and mental illness to be a homosexual then we won't be moving forward no matter how many laws we might have safeguarding the individuals.

I think this activism can be equated with feminism which advocates for equality yes initially they were opposed and hated some of the things related to this ideology but eventually, many ideas were adopted. Of course, we can argue that things are really worse but if we look at it from the time perspective, things that were controversial a couple of decades ago have now found acceptability which is a good from a certain perspective.

I see a few Indian celebrities who are known in public as homosexuals, most of them are from the Arts and Film Industry. Very rarely you would find anyone outside this coming out of the closet.

I think there are a lot of gays who have openly disclosed their sexuality to the public. I can't name them all but it is good to see that some prominent faces have come out and talked about their sexuality.

However, for a country like ours issues such as sex and homosexuality are considered taboo, and it is naturally where hard to talk about. Even on social media platforms, the acceptance rate is still not that high but then of course it is more than what we would find in real life.

There are very few openly lesbian celebrities in India compared to gays and I don't know what exactly could be the reason behind this, there is a high chance that they might have feelings towards the same gender but they are afraid to do so.

I am inquisitive to know if these women are closeted lesbians then how do they manage their everyday lives by keeping it a secret there is a lot of pressure to get married after a certain age so how does one escape this?

Are you able to tell your family that your sexuality is different, if not how does one deal with such a scenario? I mean does one get married in this scenario and you make love to someone you don't want to in the name of keeping a secret?

I don't know how hard is for lesbians in this country but I am pretty sure there are a lot of closeted lesbians, the ratio when I see homosexuals ie., gays to lesbians difference is quite. Maybe I am wrong, maybe I am a biased person who thinks that there are as many lesbians out there as gays.

I was always curious to get to know more about lesbians but then again I have yet to get in touch with them and get to know their perspective all I know of them is what I hear in the news or see on the internet.

I think it is quite unfortunate there are barely any prominent lesbian faces in India, some are rumoured to be lesbians, and some might be curious. There is however one athlete who has come out in the open.

Legally speaking I would say things have indeed become better I mean there was a time when it was criminal to say that you are gay but thankfully it is not anymore and I had read somewhere that even prominent celebrities were afraid to talk about it as they could be jailed for talking like that.

Even in urban metro areas where the acceptance rate is usually considered higher than an average family you would have a tough time making your point and forget about those tier 2 and tier 3 cities, I wonder what it would be like if their kid came out of the closet.

Even today LGBT community is a marginalised community, yes they have been given rights although marriage is still recognized only between a man and woman, there are other rights which have been provided.

The other day I was reading a document regarding LGBT rights in India, and it was interesting to see some of the rights that have been provided. I just recently learned those things existed in India.

I think from a legal perspective there is still a lot of ignorance as we don't know much about the Constitution and judiciary and there are a lot of NGOs who are working hard to make life easy.

But then again constitution might not have that much hatred against our community. They are quite open to different sexualities and there are some things even which I was not aware of as a citizen I had a right.

I think it is safe to say on paper things have changed and although same-sex marriage is not legalized still I think it is great some of the changes that have happened in the recent past and I was reading about some of the judgements in the past few years.

It is important that irrespective of whatever the identities we help each other out although I have yet to be in touch with anyone in our community in recent times which is a failure on my part.

I have been trying to fix that part because I feel guilty that I have not done enough despite coming from a financially stable background. It is not as if I was from a lower economic background then it could have been said that not much could have been done.

I have had my struggles to deal with, first accepting as my own identity and second to try and balance out my mental health which has not been great in the last few years. I had a few setbacks which have paused my life overall.

I am doing better now so I am thinking of doing some things where I try to connect with people of different sexualities and try to help them in whichever I want. I don't want them to feel abandoned by everyone around them.

Even if I am unable to help physically or mentally, I hope to offer better solutions and make them lead a more reasonable and happy life that they are leading. This is one of the biggest reasons I want this book to be published so that they get to know it in detail and maybe try to relate to my scenario and maybe create a safe space.

I know sometimes it feels impossible maybe someone who is reading this might not want to take it seriously after all I am not an organization or an influential person and anyone would first tell me to solve my problems and come out to everyone as bisexual and then solve the world's problems.

I think it is a fair point if anyone would point me that in any ideal society. But then again we don't live in an ideal society and most of us are not ideals we may have hundreds of problems in our lives but yet embark on solving other people's problems.

I have started to realize how a big hypocrite and coward I have been all my life. I know this sounds weird kind of a rant but unfortunately, it is true. I have been trying to rectify some of the mistakes of my life.

I sometimes wonder how my reaching out to some other folks might rectify my mistakes, but I feel I get that by getting in touch with these people I can get some peace. All my life I have been trying to get some mental peace.

Doing this would eventually I feel get me mental peace, yes there is no logic behind probably because when such complicated emotions things are not. At this point, I feel like I have gone a little bit off-topic with emotions.

Anyways coming to the topic, I think there are hundreds of people who are like me who may need to be made aware of certain things that most folks are not aware of.

Sometimes we think that we are alone and there is no way out.

Handling those situations can be very tense and sometimes you might need probably need a helping hand someone who is probably more suited to understand these situations and help you either legally or socially.

After all, you must have a good support system and in most cases where some problem arises you generally take immediate advice from those people who are very close to your own ie., friends, family etc.

But in such rare scenarios, we are in such a place that we can't get help and are forced to make decisions on our own. I think it's better to reach out to maybe NGOs self-help groups or therapy.

I think therapy could be great especially when you face so many dilemmas when you have tough times and have so many questions about your sexuality of late there have been many companies which have understood this need for many people.

I have been to therapy but I was there for my anxiety and I never consulted for my sexuality-related issues I think therapy could be soothing for a lot of people especially when they can vent their problems.

Instead of a knee-jerk reaction, I think this is a far better solution and it is better for those folks who want to come out to those people around them or their loved ones and dear ones. Therapy is just one of the ways if you know people who are from the same community then it is great.

You should try to support and help each other emotionally in whichever you can after all there is not much support that is there for them and eventually if both or a certain group can help each other out I think it would be great.

Recently I have been reading a lot of stuff with regards to LGBT and especially hate crimes against the group and it is kinda shocking some of the incidents that have happened in the past few years globally.

Ok, I get it there is a strong sentiment that goes against LGBT and it might be against your religion and culture in certain geographical conditions there are traditionalists who consider it morally wrong and unnatural and I may not understand the sentiment but yes I can accept that that kind of people exists but what I don't get is the kind of hatred a certain group is getting.

Yes you don't like a certain group, who you feel are like a piece of shit or something that might not be ok but for the sake of argument I might understand that these kinds of people exist but to understand that those people who want to just dead that is some serious stuff.

I don't think I can find justification for this, I mean I have tried hard to find the reasoning behind this hatred and how killing someone solves their problem because I like to get their perspectives even though I dislike the entire idea.

But I cannot see any justification behind this hatred for the execution of gays and it is, to be frank, a waste of time discussing with them as they come up with one ridiculous thing after another and they would never give you a straight answer.

They would engage in fear-mongering that gays have taken over this and that and they would eventually corrupt youth and eventually everyone would become gay or lesbian which is a matter of concern for them as it will corrupt a generation.

Strangely, a lot of hatred comes from a fear that there is a certain minority group and eventually, they would take over everything and all of society will be destroyed if they are not stopped I think this is indeed a strange fear for any individual to have.

Now logically you can argue that if let's say someone comes out as a homosexual after seeing someone I think that is a good thing. If he/ she were to keep it hidden all their life I think the amount of pain and struggle they had to go through for this is certainly immeasurable and with a little bit of decent exposure if they can come out of this trap I think it is great.

No one should be punished for speaking their mind, yes in the past this might have happened but just because this has happened in the past that doesn't mean that it should keep happening again and again.

One common argument that has been constantly thrown for centuries is that homosexuality is unnatural so it means that it goes against the law of nature and to go against it means that you are committing a very big mistake and there are consequences for it.

But here is the problem with the theory that there have been many different animals which display this sort of behaviour, no one went and told them to behave in this certain way and yet these animals display this kind of behaviour.

Oddly, these animals who were supposed to behave in a certain way started behaving in an abnormal way of life which goes against the law of nature. These animals have been displaying such behaviour for many centuries and even though they were around us we didn't bother that much.

When the truth came out we didn't accept it, we thought it was a lie told by the researchers to suit their agenda after all that was not what was told to us when we were kids and now we are being told that some animals might exhibit naturally and they have been doing so for thousands for years if not more.

Since they are now out of ideas they come out with a new theory that god does not like homosexuals and he would not like it if anyone comes out as a homosexual as it is a very disgusting thing to do.

Now this trick is neat and very appealing to a lot of people, it makes you feel that you are a bad person if you commit such a thing and there is fear among an individual or community they start to feel it is a disgusting thing to do and no one should do it and if you indulge in such an activity you are a bad person doing a bad thing.

It works like a charm when you add a little bit of a religious angle to it after all there are so many things which we are not aware of and one such thing is life after death and this is where I suppose there is a unanimous agreement over almost every culture.

There are many common factors which you can find which might be the same for different cultures such as love, fear of god, marriage, the concept of sin, heaven and hell etc and you can find hatred against homosexuality is one such thing you would find that it is a common thing.

Probably that is the reason, homophobia is not just limited to one region but is there globally there might be hundreds of differences between those cultures but there are some common factors which are the same everywhere.

I don't know who that person who came up with the idea that homosexuality is unnatural was either not well-read or had some ulterior motives because he clearly could not understand what being natural means or he was not aware of the animals exhibited such behaviour.

I think it is very strange that we live in a time where we have to still give proof of everything and despite giving all the proof it is never enough for the other side. We somehow end on the losing side and they would eventually win all the battles and decide what's right and wrong.

It is funny that people talk about the greatness of love and respect and how love triumphs over hate but then again they have problems against whom we have love and now we have to justify this how it is normal and we don't have a disease.

I feel almost sick that now we have to prove that what we are doing has to be justified to each of the critics. It must be tough for others to conduct their day-to-day life as the existing drama is so much that you can barely think straight.

There is not much we can do I can guess I mean we are not the lawmakers and even if all the lawmakers become like us it would not be much of a difference because unfortunately, the mob mentality is such a way that as an individual you would behave differently but as a group you behave like a bully.

Maybe those people who hate us and want us to vanish just hate our guts that we could be what we want and they do not have any option but they are dictated by someone else what they can do and what they cannot.

And just when they see that someone is not going as per the normal standards they become moral police and start their moral policing thinking that if they do not do something bad will happen eventually leading to some kind of catastrophe which would have an overall bad situation so to do so such things have to be stopped.

I know it is kind of crazy to apprehend what I just said and maybe to some of you it would not make sense but that is the exact problem because no one knows what goes through their mind. We can only speculate even if you try to have a normal conversation you end up having more questions.

On the internet, they come up with such bizarre logic that one cannot understand if they have gone full retard just trying to say stuff which makes no sense sometimes I feel pity for them and mostly I don't feel anything for them because they are ruthless in their online trolling which I am not supportive of.

I am sure there are others as well who have experienced this as well, as internet bullying is something which I have often felt is a thing which happens to a lot of folks belonging to different sections of people no matter where you come from.

LGBT community is one such community which often gets bullied online and as a result, there is a lot of trauma and stress which I have faced personally so much that I had to quit a social media platform so when you are outnumbered and the odds are not in a favour you often feel helpless and sometimes you may feel lonely and end up doing this which you may regret later in your life.

We talk about lgbt rights on one hand and the reality is most folks have a tough time coming out freely and being themselves and every day feels like a struggle where those questions don't end, sometimes it just feels like we have committed some kind of crime and we are being investigated daily.

Now and then you try to avoid questions, you try to justify how you are doing ok and then people want you to fail so that they come up with the expression told you so and you didn't listen to me which is kind of irritating and makes me wanna punch in the face.

I am not really a violent person but then sometimes situations can make you feel frustrated that you want an exit from all of this and at times I feel tired physically and mentally from all this crap. You think that you have seen it all and then the next day it becomes even worse, there are good and bad days.

It is safe to say that the bad days heavily outnumber good days, this is just my personal opinion I mean I could be wrong may be I think that situation is really bad from what I have seen and heard from the things around me.

Maybe I am a delusional guy who thinks that the LGBT community is at risk from a certain set of individuals and they need to be protected from all this moral policing and useless lectures. I have never really had a problem being wrong and I hope I am wrong from a long distance.

After all, it would be great if all the stuff I am thinking about mental health and fear about sexuality was only inside my head but I think there is a little bit of reality to it. If people from the LGBT community are living a great life and I am the only one who thinks that these kinds of things happen then I would be happy to be proven wrong.

I think I am from being delusional and I can see the truth times I can read between the lines which unfortunately I am very good at. It is one skill I keep asking myself whether or not I have because at times it is so good to be true and it is indeed a tragedy for my life.

Speaking of tragedies, we don't talk about how they affect different individuals, especially in a country like ours where you just cannot accept different sexualities and the kind of comments that we receive I mean they are truly horrible and I honestly don't know how these social media companies allow these accounts to be active.

On one hand, they talk about diversity and inclusion and how hate speech is not tolerated by these big companies. They just talk big, they are well aware of the fact that if we are to remove every user who makes homophobic statements then there would be hardly any people who are left to use their platform so they turn a blind eye to it.

So for these companies, money plays an important role and it is quite clear that they have sorted their priorities no matter how many times I would report their profile their accounts could not be stopped and they would stop at nothing.

Their comments are not only vile but are very distasteful and now someone would say that it is best to block those kinds of people but I am a human and can only block a few accounts. What can you do if they create alt accounts almost every day and come to harass me?

I was at times feeling helpless I tried all the things that could be done and I failed miserably eventually it was too much for me to take and I had to quit because bullying was in such a high number that it was starting to affect my health.

Both my physical and mental health was starting to deteriorate because of the said things and one might wonder yes people can be cruel online. We are supposed to ignore such vile things and carry forward and not care about them but I think it was hard for me to just ignore it because some or the other way it was affecting my opinions and the way I used to think.

It was a turning point for me, very few people knew me and yet I had to face so much harassment for I do not know what crime I had ever committed. Gay slurs were often used in the most horrible all my arguments were shut down saying that I suck cock so my opinion is inferior to others.

Even though on paper LGBT rights look good people from the other side might point out things which might make it seem that we are well protected and guarded. Initially, I was also under the impression that we are better than most of the countries when it comes to LGBT rights.

I was wrong in so many ways I was starting to realize that the system fails quite frequently and there is a lot of injustice that is being done and so much that people have eventually given up because the other side is too strong to reckon with.

I now understand how things work in my country, there is a theory of all the rules that are there what should happen and what should not happen and then there is the reality which is quite the opposite of the theory and usually, theory and reality often don't match and it is frustrating for not me but for a lot of people.

Now and then I see people around me complain so much about the judiciary and how the system has failed them from time and I could not understand why they would say such a thing. Yes, our system is a bit slow but because it does not want to punish innocents in the pursuit of that we end up losing a lot of innocence.

I can now understand their frustration a little bit although our battles are completely different I feel there is a similarity in situations in which we have ended up together and we see things in such a way that even though the system looks so good on paper it has delivered probably the worst results.

Now if someone faces a similar dilemma then there could be several reasons why they would feel that way after all the rights we give to our citizens are very well thought and if someone feels they don't have any rights at all then there must be some problem.

And if someone who does not come from my community claims a similar problem maybe a problem does exist with our society as well as the system that serves justice. I know that this might be considered offensive but then again I have to be truthful here.

We all have faced some sort of injustice which makes us feel that there could be never any justice done. A lot of people might still have hope in our system and law while the others don't which is a very complicated scenario.

Often folks who believe justice will not be served are countered by the facts that despite the flaws still it is not as bad as it seems to be and we can always give it a second chance. I have not been a victim of a failed system but a rather failed society that can understand why some are losing faith and maybe it is a bad thing.

Maybe I am just imagining stuff again and everything is great i mean the people have been granted rights by our constitution and everything is set in a manner that justice can be done to everyone maybe people in the judiciary think that way and maybe they are right from their perspective.

Their intentions might be really good and the major reason why the rights are great on paper but somehow people are unable to encash them is probably because they are not aware of them. Even if they are aware of it they are in such a situation that they might be overpowered by people who are just too stubborn.

The other day I was reading an article where some foreign journalist had written a piece on LGBT rights in India and he thought that 377 is gone and it is a major relief despite all the rights and clauses still a long way to go for justice.

Yes, we are going in the right direction still a lot of changes have to come and they have to be enforced in such a way that people can accept these folks as their own without hating them or wanting to kill each other. I feel there has to be extensive marketing to normalise otherwise even after 100 years we would be still debating the same things which we are doing now.

IV
Homophobia

Homophobia according to the Oxford Dictionary is defined as negative attitudes towards homosexuals and homosexuality which may be manifested in discrimination, hostile behaviour, and hate crimes although this definition can be added to bisexuals and transgenders.

We have discussed some of these aspects in the previous chapters, I started the chapter by writing the definition of it because I wanted to make it clear what I mean by the term homophobia every time I use it because on the internet people dismiss it as nothing.

For them, it seems like another word which seems to be created by us to create confusion and diversion among the people but the word is there to tell people what kind of behaviour they are exhibiting and how it is affecting an entire community through that discrimination or stereotypes which are being propagated.

It is hard to tell where to start on this topic because homophobia is pretty much everywhere and I don't know where it has originated. If it was started because in the past homosexuals didn't exist I am afraid that is untrue and there have been several people in the past and even during the era of kings and queens such people existed.

So the logic that there were no such people in past and that these kinds of people have started to exist in recent times is a completely fabricated lie. Sometimes it feels like we are living in times of polarizing views you can be either be extremist of this kind or that kind.

It is sad to see the labels that are being thrown at each other from both sides. We throw labels and we do not want to discuss there are certain areas we don't want to go and even if we go there by chance we just throw racist or supremacist jibes.

Yes, racist and supremacist people do exist but the rate at which those jibes get thrown at each other is very idiotic. People could disagree with you on certain topics and might not have said something racist or stuff that is supremacist but eventually they get labelled and once you get labelled the game is pretty much over.

The problem with the labels is that they can dodge the argument using that label so I think it is extremely important unless that person displays those characteristics we should not simply throw labels at the other person otherwise they might react crudely.

The reason I am stressing out about it is that I want to engage more and more people. The more we can engage with them the more we can make them feel the kind of behaviour they are displaying, this might not affect a lot of people but even if we can change a few people's behaviours and make them realize how their behaviour I think it is still a good situation for us.

I still have high hopes for this current generation although the previous couple of generations are lost for me. There is no way in this world you could fight with them because no matter how hard you try they have closed their minds a long time ago and it is really hard to convince someone who has closed their minds.

Although the arguments I had over them were with other topics making my point was still hard compared to the younger generation who were more open to ideas. It feels like you are talking to an open book there is a chance of going forth and back and you can be hopeful that even if they are not getting it today maybe in future they might understand it once they think hard about it.

I think I am correct in assessing the newer generation as they are less rigid compared to the older generation so I would rather have these kinds of talks with the newer generation who are more likely to open up with these thoughts and are ready to hear your point of view even though they might not like your point of view.

I think the newer generation does not hate homosexuals compared to the previous generation, they have much more tolerance towards them. Of course, not everyone is like this but this is the general perception I have when I see them engage with others or myself in random conversations.

There might be several individuals who hate homosexuals but this generation is at least ready to debate and wants to hear the other side and then make an opinion based on that as opposed to prefixing your mind in such a way that you start to think that you know everything already and whatever the other person tells to you is plain stupid talk.

The main point is that if you can make those kids hear this side of the story and make them understand that we are not your enemies but people who are different from yours then maybe the future might be better for us.

Our lives have not been great, most of us have been in hiding for the right reasons but if the coming generations don't hate this community and accept it as our own despite the differences they have with us I think it will be a great victory for us as a community.

At least those folks in the future who would want to identify as homosexual or bisexual or any other gender identity will be in a society where people would not be afraid to hide their sexuality and come out in the open and only then we can say that we have progressed in our mission.

We must educate people around us especially kids of the newer generation before someone sows the seeds of hate because humans are in a way like plants and whichever way you grow it will eventually grow in that direction, so our message must go to teenagers, young adults and if possible we can tell it to people who are middle age or older.

With proper education maybe we can tackle the problem of homophobia which is quite frankly rampant everywhere it can be found in day-to-day conversation in academia or on the internet. These kinds of slurs are thrown randomly at us irrespective of religion or gender.

We can find this homophobia in movies, stand-up comedy, comics, entertainment etc. It is a common theme you can find across all the different sections of society where they might have disagreements on hundreds of issues but they have a unanimous agreement over homosexuality.

Let's start with academics because school is an essential part of any kid's life. Whatever he/she learns might be embedded in his mind for the rest of his life, so it is important whatever the stuff that is being taught concerning homosexuality.

Unfortunately, there is no formal education or teaching that is being taught to kids to ensure that they understand the different sexualities and identities that are there. When you do not get that kind of education from your syllabus, naturally, you will have to rely on your classmates or your seniors where they share their knowledge with you.

The one big tragedy with this is if the kid is studying in any ordinary school, what I mean by the ordinary school is that school which is not an international school. If the kid is working at the school then there is a high chance that you would be told how homosexuals are unnatural people with some kind of mental illness and how they should avoid such people if they want to stay out of trouble.

I think childhood is one place where the seeds of hatred against homosexuality are sown and we often ignore we tend to focus more on young adults and educate them but it is really hard to educate someone who has been hearing so much against homosexuality they start to feel that is indeed the reality.

Unfortunately, the propaganda machine works so well that even if you would like to keep an open mind you would fall for their propaganda and start hating homosexuals for no reason. I would say there are many victims of this propaganda and it is important that this propaganda system needs to be abolished.

I know saying this is easy but doing it is very hard, after all, we don't have many resources to accomplish what I am trying to say and in fact, most folks would feel that it is a waste of time to think about educating the kids and not to mention it would be considered a breach of privacy as we cannot access their kids just the way we want.

The parents have first right to their kids and they can teach their kids whatever religious or spiritual education they feel is right for them to their kids and if we try to impose any of our beliefs we might face trouble for that.

I know it would be nearly impossible for us to do these kinds of things and whichever NGOs are working for the betterment of LGBT do not have this as their priority but

I still wish that whoever is working on these can spare a moment for this suggestion.

Although I am a nobody when it comes to LGBT activism still I think I can offer something to the community even though I cannot do much hopefully we can focus on those things which truly affect society and school is one such place which truly can be a game changer.

Even if we can't focus on schools maybe we can focus on colleges and since the kids in college are usually around 18 years if we can focus on the kids who are taking college irrespective of their ideology if we can convince even a few of them regarding homophobia I think it would be great news for us.

Of course, it is not easy and giving suggestions is much easier than doing the deed but I think we never focused in this area. All our life we have faced so much criticism for our identities that we have been trying to breathe all along and try to survive in society and maybe it is time we focus on other things which can yield good results.

Sometimes all it takes is a good idea from someone which can spark something and might even set the stage for us and we might not have to look back. Right now we as a community need to stall a little bit and think what our next movement should be for like next 2-3 decades.

Having this kind of talk regularly will establish us with the ground reality and it is important to make progress from time to time. I wish I was in a situation and people under me so that I could be part of that change but I am trying to help in any way I can.

It is true that I am at the end of the day a powerless guy whose only strong weapon is his words and if reading this brings some changes to your life or you can work for a change or the betterment of the community I think I have succeeded in doing something wonderful and it might have a good impact overall from my perspective.

I have been lenient and lazy for most of my life and there are many things that I would like to change currently, I am working on a few things. Hopefully, there will come a time when I can contribute to the community and then I will finally feel that I have done really for the community and it will give me immense joy and pleasure.

I was always interested in knowing folks who can understand my point of view and want to do the same thing as I do. I would be fascinated to meet other people from the LGBT community and get to know their feedback irrespective of wherever they might belong.

Hopefully, this book gets published and can reach a wider audience, I would be really curious to know how they view this book what the similarities and differences in their life while reading this book and if they disagree on certain things which I have said.

I would be interested to know the feedback and if I have been wrong in some places I would be happy to get corrected by someone after all this is a learning thing for me and I do not know everything I would be happy to be shown the truth and I would be glad to be corrected no matter who.

I think after academic institutions one source where different kinds of people are influenced in huge numbers is cinema. Movies are loved by a large number of people and often we see stereotypical representations sometimes they show us in such a bad light it might even invoke strong feelings against them which is not a good thing.

This thing has been going on for several decades and many of the stereotypes have not only been established by mainstream movies irrespective of language but they continue to haunt several of us.

Some of those stereotypes have been so brutal that it has marked us forever, every time that character on screen has been targeted it feels like a personal attack. Sometimes I could imagine myself instead of that character and it saddens me when such scenes are celebrated.

Homosexuals are shown as cowards who are not man enough and eventually, this creates an impression in the mind of young that is true because no one is there to counter your arguments and because the lie has been repeated so many times it eventually becomes truth and everyone starts to believe in those lies.

I guess that is how propaganda works and has been successful. I remember as a kid how I used to feel disgusted by homosexuals and how they were the scum of the planet. I never wanted to kill them but I had hatred in my brain for them and I don't know what would have happened if I continued to believe this which was constantly being fed to me.

I was a very peaceful person since childhood rarely getting in fights with other people, if the propaganda had such an impact on me then imagine the kind of impact it could have on an aggressive person they might even want to physically harm that person and we hear a lot of cases in the news.

It is tough for me to imagine the kind of trauma one person has to go through if they are physically beaten just for being homosexual or any other sexuality. That person might be broken from the inside and he might feel helpless and no one might even feel for that person, it is such a horrible situation to be in.

It is hard to say how much movies have created trouble for us since there has been no research conducted on how our psyche has been shaped towards homosexuals based on the movies we watch especially where the characters that a homosexual or any other sexuality are a bit different from society's standards.

Now some folks always come in defence of movies every time there is a controversy regarding movies where there are allegations movies inspire hate or violence against a particular community especially the LGBT community and their only defence is that movies are meant for entertainment and are targeted unnecessarily.

I agree that movies are for entertainment but in our country we are crazy for 2 things one is movies and the other is cricket. Movies are almost like a religion here and the heroes are like gods we worship them and it is quite evident from the craze for movies we see that how much movies are important in someone's life.

Call me crazy for believing this but I think the movies play a great role, just like they can have a positive impact they can have a negative impact as well. When a movie with a good impact releases we all praise that and try to correlate with reality how a certain movie is bringing a change within society and share real-life examples.

When we do that we are acknowledging the fact that there is a strong impact of movies on its audience, especially the younger generation who have a tough time controlling their emotions under control and might get carried away.

These are the impressionable boys and girls and may believe whatever you show them, they are not scientists every time you show something they might do research and give feedback because that is how young minds work and filmmakers knowingly or unknowingly try to take advantage of that.

They try to impose their ideas subtly and no I am no conspiracy theorist who wants to make claims so far from the movies I have seen in my life it is quite evident that every film-maker has his ideology and at times they are ready to go to any lengths to get his point across which is my basic argument.

They can make an argument which might be controversial or something which is not accepted by a lot of folks look good through cinematic liberties and finesse. There might be an event they might be making a movie on and they would be presenting it from a certain perspective.

Since most of the movies are a work of fiction and every time you question they hide behind the argument that we are not defaming anybody or any community we are just doing this for entertainment but I think it is quite clear that they are doing with an agenda. I am not saying all movies are like this but some of them are made with this intention sometimes to even whitewash or gaslight a specific community.

Sadly, so many of the movies have anti-LGBT themes in them movies and some of them even justify how being homosexual is equivalent to a disease in mainstream movies these movies are then watched and loved by millions of people and now that subtle reference becomes the main point.

More and more this theme is shown to the audience and the more a particular community is laughed at, mocked at and has been subjected to other kinds of harassment. I am not suggesting that movies are entirely responsible for the mess we are in right now but they have played a major part in homophobia.

I think movies have not only played a major part in homophobia but also have a major role in normalizing eve-teasing which is even more shocking than anything. When I used to hear arguments that movies are responsible for rising violence against women by certain people I refused to believe it but slowly I started understanding things.

Of course, no one on this planet can prove that movies are motivating people of the younger generation or anybody in general to commit a violent crime. If somebody could prove it maybe things would have been different and there would have been more pressure on filmmakers while choosing their content.

But not all films are alike, slowly things are changing there has been good representation when it comes to movies with LGBT themes. I think those movies and their creators should be appreciated for their attempt I guess although the number of movies is such a small number.

One can argue that when there are movies made with LGBT themes things are balanced out but unfortunately, that is not true. Movies with LGBT themes receive a lot of criticism and they don't run successfully compared to movies with anti LGBT themes.

Recently there has been criticism of movies with LGBT themes and it is really unfortunate the hate it receives. The ironic thing movies where homosexuals are treated as shit no one has a problem but in the movies where the representation is slightly better not only receive criticism but also receive hate.

Some of the criticism those movies get is ridiculous and there are a lot of conspiracy theories that through these movies filmmakers want to brainwash the younger generation into becoming homosexual. A lot of them think that filmmakers have an agenda while making these kinds of movies and want to influence a whole lot of people.

I think these films can be a boon to a lot of people who have nowhere else to go. It could be a ray of hope to folks who are lonely and might have complicated feelings towards all things. I think these kinds of movies should at least be encouraged by our community because at times watching those kinds of movies and TV shows makes me emotional as it is hard for me to believe that it is possible to show us in good light.

Apart from academia and films, another place that is a source where a lot of homophobia exists is the workplace. The last job I worked on was filled with these kinds of people so it became really difficult to work there especially when you are a closeted bisexual. I was afraid at times that my secret would be discovered someday and I don't know how they would react to it.

I am sure folks who don't reveal themselves to be homosexuals face this kind of anxiety and it might start to affect on work they are doing and eventually it might hamper their productivity. I honestly don't know what guidelines are laid out by corporate companies for LGBT people and even if there are companies which care they might be in tiny proportion.

A lot of folks in our country are homophobic which explains why we have such hate crimes against our community and it is surprising that some of the comments they receive. What's more shocking is the fact that ancient India had some prominent people who were not heterosexuals so a country with such a history has now come to this.

I am curious to know what are the things that transpired to us as a society who were welcoming people of different sexualities to absolutely shunning and discarding them as pieces of shit. These kinds of things don't happen overnight and there might be something in the past which might be able to help us understand why this might have happened.

There are many theories on the internet and it is hard to believe which one is accurate, some seem like conspiracy theories while others are not so convincing some are even childish and funny and I will not go into the details as I feel it is unnecessary right.

Whatever the reasons, I think it is safe to say that we changed. Our society does change whether you like it or not, I know there are some naysayers but eventually, you have the newer generation with newer ideas.

So I think it is safe to say irrespective of what others might think even though at one part of the time we were accepting of homosexuals ultimately a new idea emerged which then started to feel threatened by us and a lot of us were persecuted just by the people of those times who thought we were indulging in some sort of crime.

There was no concept of democracy, rights and judiciary back then and even if it did exist it was in the hands of one person or a few groups of people and you could not question them as it would lead to strict punishment or death in some cases.

We are now no longer living in those king's era where one man would decide my fate. Our way of living has changed at that time the kings used to do whatever their advisors used to tell them but now things are not like that. No one can impose his/ her ideology onto your throat.

We have police, law and courts and we have NGOs that could help us other methods might help you if you feel that you have been treated unfairly by a group or by an individual. Of course, we have many flaws and often we might not be getting what we deserve but I think the situation is much better if we compare it to a few centuries ago when no one would listen to us and would be executed if we were exposed.

Anyway, I am glad that I was born in an era where different ideas and ideologies are accepted and even experimented and there is freedom of speech as well these things are very crucial for our times.

I still think that I have a lot of hopes for the newer generation no matter how the situation might be right now I think eventually the older generation would die and it is up to the newer generation where they want this whole fiasco to go.

Do they want to commit the same mistakes their forefathers have been making or do they want a fresh start and try to build a new society where acceptance exists for people like me?   I think a lot of it is dependent on those people, especially heterosexuals because they outnumber us in very large numbers.

We have been fighting for centuries and in the future also we will continue to do the same. Some of us might fight, some of us might give but the movement will still be there. The folks would be ready to give it all for their community.

The folks who would be defending might be different but they will be there and I am pretty confident that our community will eventually grow more and more in numbers. Eventually, our voices and our concerns will be heard we shall be able to manage at least to live a life without getting bothered by so many questions.

We have so many people around us who question their sexuality, I think it is important that those people whether they are kids or teenagers, young adults or even older people should be able to reach out to the right people.

When someone faces a complex problem, usually they confide in loved ones but the issue is such that even the utterance of such things can cause fear in your mind as you are afraid of how these people are going to react and what might happen to me if they get to know my sexuality.

I am sure this is a dilemma a lot of young people might face and they don't know where to go even therapy could be very expensive. Yes there are a lot of start-ups nowadays which focus on therapy and they claim to focus on LGBT but I still think there are a lot of folks who just cannot afford it.

You cannot talk to your family or therapy and the only kind of people you want to talk to are your friends which is again 50-50 for me because we don't know the kind of mentality they have or how they are going to react about it. If you have friends who support you in your decision I think that you are lucky, at least I wasn't this lucky when it comes to my circle of friends.

I always felt a fear that if they discovered my identity they would eventually feel disgusted by me and stop talking to me I would be isolated and alienated by my friends and my teachers and the school would eventually rusticate me and no school would ever take me as a student due to my past behaviour.

I don't know how many people in their high school got to know about their sexuality but yes I was one of the few who experienced it at a very young age and I knew it so well that I could not just tell anyone and I had to be careful wherever I go I could not be whatever I want it to be.

A decade later I am still wondering about the consequences of getting exposed, I think we are much safer now but there is this one fear of alienation by everyone if it becomes a reality. People don't like homosexuals so my neighbours might not appreciate me as a guy living near them and would want me to vacate the premises.

It is easy for anyone to come out of their closet online rather than offline because, in the real world, there are consequences which do not apply to the online world. You can block someone in the online world but you cannot do the same thing with your neighbour.

You will have to bear him/her for many many years and both of you might hate each other and there might be fights and arguments happening and eventually, he will keep reminding your sexuality every now and I think we all are afraid of getting judged whether we will accept it or not.

As I said earlier I am really afraid of my sexuality being out in the open I think I might be alienated further which I do not want at the present moment. I think I will keep it a secret for a while until I feel safe then I will eventually reveal it to everyone until then I will watch my back and make sure that no one finds out my secret.

If I had a born in a Western country maybe things would have been different but then again you won't get to choose where you are born so I will have to adjust to what I have. I know that I am not alone and hopefully others can connect with me maybe I will feel good if they share their stories with me I think it might be a booster for me because at times I feel bad about myself.

V

Pride Parade

I never really liked the idea of the Pride Parade, I thought it was a forced concept on my community we might be doing a disservice to our people by doing these kinds of things so I have never gone to an actual Pride parade even though I have been a part of this community for so long.

To be frank I never really understood the concept of community thing I have discovered it recently because most of the time I never felt like I belonged to someone or some group. I have always considered myself to be a loner and I didn't have any problem with that because I like being alone but I do not feel lonely because I think those are two different things.

I am not going to explain the difference now this is not a philosophical lecture. But now I have started to realize that I have to be part of some or the other community especially when I identify as bisexual it is important for me to connect with others like me or at least try to connect with them.

I might not need them but a lot of folks might need me and eventually, I would be able to learn some new things because that is the beauty of socializing with similar interests can make you feel. It feels like you are with the right person and we might be able to express our emotions and we would not be judged for our actions.

Now I am starting to realize that I am part of this community whether I like it or not. People would judge me for being part of this community and that is understandable up to one extent anyone would associate me with a certain group.

I am not ashamed to be what I am and I have realized that no matter how much I try to escape the tags and labels I would not be able to escape it. People will label me no matter how hard I try not to get myself labelled.

I think it is time that I stop running from everything and accept myself and my sexuality and also accept that I am part of this community even though I am not the best when it comes to making relationships I still think that I need to develop some connections within this community or get to know those folks who are supportive of LGBT community.

All my life I have surrounded myself with folks who hate homosexuals or people with other sexual identities and I was pretty much okay with it. For the first time, I feel that I should surround myself with people who are either supportive of that or get involved with people who are from the LGBT community.

I would be really glad to meet folks who are LGBT from my city or are from any other place around the world. I think folks who hate LGBT have been spreading a lot of negativity recently and for change, I would be interested in knowing another point of view.

Frankly speaking, I have not yet met a lesbian in my real life and I was very curious to meet someone one day. It is not that I have bad intentions it is just that curiosity is kinda killing and I want to know what it is like being a lesbian in India and what are the challenges they have faced in their academics and professional life.

To date, I have only my perspective which is great so far but having my perspective is not enough I think I would need people from different sexualities. There might be folks who don't like their gender and would like to change their genders i would want to meet them as well.

I would be interested to hear their stories and I would also like to narrate my stories and take their feedback overall because I believe it helps in growing myself as a person. I don't have much experience in this area, but I would like to become an expert.

I know that this is not easy and it takes years of hard work and patience but I think it is worth the try and that is when I realized why the pride parade was important. A lot of folks think that it is a nuisance to create some drama but I don't think that is the case.

These kinds of parades are extremely important to us because in a way it is used to represent that we exist and we are not some lunatics who live here and there and slowly we are coming out in the open whether you like it or not.

You might hate us for our sexuality and might not want to accept us for who we are but that doesn't matter. There was a time when we used to be in fear and there was a lot of panic about what could happen to us but that is not true anymore. We are stronger than before and our community is getting stronger and better.

We are not here to intimidate anyone but to show that we are now an essential part of this very society and those days are gone we used to feel ashamed of ourselves and our sexual orientation and felt like there is no hope for tomorrow.

I think our battles are different and despite all our differences, we are eventually one. Our sexualities might be different and a lot of us have faced trauma it is not comparable to talk about one trauma with the other because that would be very disrespectful from my end but I think at the end of the day we can support and help each other in whatever we can because no one else is going to save us we have to save ourselves.

I haven't been in a parade but I can understand the sentiment behind it and fully endorse it wholeheartedly. I know there is a lot of criticism for those kinds of parades as they keep telling us to keep our sexualities private and they don't care as long as we keep it private.

The problem with that argument is that they never stay out of our sexualities or our preferences, there is constant moral policing when it comes to us and they want us to think that we are the loud ones who are who have no other work to do but to create drama.

This is such an idiotic thing to believe and whoever believes that needs a reality check. We have been forced to explain our sexuality and have been forced to give logic behind everything we do. Our lives have been to a large extent compromised and we were forced to go into hiding to change ourselves.

It is absurd that despite all this happening to us as a community, the other side keeps levelling baseless allegations that we should keep our sexuality, I don't think they understand the reality here. The reality is in fact opposite of what they say, they have been snooping around in other people's beds so much with their faces and questioning everyone who doesn't act like them and now when everything is out in the open they act innocent.

I think this whole coming out in public is a good thing for us because no matter what happens whether the other person accepts your sexuality or not it does not matter but what matters is that you have to be truthful and somewhere down the line I have not been completely truthful that is why I am a very big hypocrite.

I know it is quite sad that those words are coming out of my mouth but they are true, I have been a hypocrite all my life and I think it is high time I acknowledge and at times I have been very homophobic which is not good at all but I have realized it much later in life.

I am glad that I have realized it and that is why I value Pride Parades so much I think they are a great way to express yourself and tell the world what you are. You might always feel that someone is watching you or hearing and you cannot do whatever you like but there comes a time when you can forget it for some time.

You can finally shout in joy and proclaim your freedom, the freedom to express yourself, love anyone, be intimate with anyone, and do what you feel is right.

I know that a lot of folks would be wondering how going to the pride parade solves such a huge problem. Yes you are right going to a parade will not solve your problems but it gives hope and hope is a great problem-solver. You might not be able to have all the solutions but you may start to have a positive mind which is crucial.

I think having a positive mind is crucial to whatever you are doing. I am not saying it specifically with a certain problem but with any problem, you must have a positive mind, if you can have a positive mind you can certainly achieve anything.

It is the mindset which counts which I have realized quite recently I have been keeping an open mind to a lot of things and it is keeping me healthy physically and mentally. I think both community and pride parades are crucial to our mental health.

I am not a mental health expert dealing with the LGBT community but I have written my heart, hopefully, whether you are pro-LGBT or anti-LGBT you will try to understand without trying to diss me too much and even if there is some criticism of my writing hopefully it will be constructive criticism.

I am not a fan of criticism which makes personal remarks because I hate it when someone makes personal remarks just based on what I have written. They assume things that I have done in my personal life and come to conclusions with their imagination.

Anyway I am always surprised there are very few pride parades in India, I think the main reason is that it is really hard to get permission and there would be very few takers for this parade. I see folks who are not from the LGBT community who support LGBT more in these kinds of parades than the LGBT community.

I guess a lot of folks don't want their face to be seen which can be dangerous to their life and can threaten their day-to-day activities if someone spots them in some news channel. That is my theory if I am wrong please let me know the actual truth behind it.

So far from what I have seen this is the only conclusion I see, most of the folks are afraid to come to this parade including me and I think the more and more these parades are increased the more we can get people to come out to join this parade.

I know it is quite a dangerous thing to say but using masks while attending this parade can be something which can help you to stay anonymous after all I don't think in the name of LGBT unity we should risk showing any person for which he/ she might have to face consequences later.

We might be at our homes relaxing but the other person who has shown their face might be in trouble with their family or the place they live and might have to face social alienation just because he came and showed his face to the world and that would be very disturbing for me and in a way I would have destroyed one life unknowingly.

I know arranging pride parades is not easy I guess and that is the reason you see so many pride parades annually even if those parades happen they are limited to big metropolitan cities while the other smaller cities just have to wait for our turn.

I know this is sometimes frustrating that I feel that I am not doing enough as an individual but then I say to myself that this is the best I can do because, at the end of the day, I have my limitations. It is not that I am very rich and powerful that I can change the course of things whichever way I want.

Most days I feel hopeless powerless and vulnerable and I hate those moments when I am at my weakest. I don't like to admit it but I hate these moments and I just want to alienate myself from the rest of the world and not show how weak I am.

There are days I wish that I was very rich and powerful, I am not much of a dreamer but I guess for a change I would like to dream about being rich and powerful. If I were really rich and powerful then I would use all the things possible to make sure that I can create a safe space for LGBT.

Unfortunately, I am also in the rat race to survive so ultimately my priority is to make sure that I am alive and healthy both physically and mentally and when I am good on my own then I should help others and give it back to society in whichever I can.

I am starting to realize that maybe both things can be done simultaneously although I need to prioritize and based on that we can move forward. Both my personal life and activism can be done side by side given that I can cater equal time for both.

Pride parades signify a lot of things, we tend to think that it is just to show the world what we are as a community but it is more than that. It also signifies and reminds us that we are challenging societal norms which want us to accept traditional roles.

The very idea that you are only attracted to the opposite gender is absurd. There are different sexualities around the world but to think that only if you are attracted to the opposite gender it is a rightful thing and anything other than that is sinful is quite absurd.

Not only are you setting standards for what should be accepted or not accepted, but you are also not allowing people of other sexualities to freely practice their sexualities which is totally against the idea of free speech. These sorts of moral policing are a way of bullying where you are forcing the other way to accept certain things.

I think they are wrong if they want to dictate our sex lives, I don't think anyone has the right to decide my sex life as long as I am doing it consensually with an adult. That's the golden rule right whichever part of the world you might live you would more or less would have to live by this code of conduct.

If you feel that there should be a group that should get to decide whether or not homosexuality or some other sexuality is valid or not, I think that would be called moral policing. Today they are discussing immorality regarding homosexuality, tomorrow there might be other topics that might be discussed such as clothes you can wear, and things you can believe in.

I think this is quite a dangerous trend and we should not encourage it. It does not matter whether or not you are homosexual or not, this is about freedom to choose and live and we are not living in a dictator land where just because someone does not like something it has to be banned completely.

Anyone who strongly believes that ideas should be enforced down the throats of other people, they are indeed enemies of our democracy. They don't believe in the idea of free speech and they don't know what freedom stands for.

I have come across a lot of folks who display such characteristics, even the word homosexual makes them feel disgusted and they react in such a way that homosexuals don't have a right to live. I think everyone has a right to live just because someone is disgusted doesn't mean that they should be dead.

No human should get that much power that they decide who is allowed to live and who is not. I think we all are humans and we have different approaches to life. Our philosophy towards a lot of things varies from person to person.

The human population on Earth is more than 8 billion and nearly 75 percent of the population is aged above 15 years so it is safe to say around 6 billion people who are at the age of 15 years or more.

I think once you have reached the age of 15, you are smart enough that you can figure out things on your own and not everyone needs to subscribe to the same set of things just you do.

Everyone has their brain so they will agree to some things while they might disapprove of certain things which they might not like or hate you are still on good terms even though they are disagreeing. I think it should be applied to the LGBT community as well, when you don't hate someone just because you disagree I don't think you should hate just because we are different.

Pride Parades ultimately tell the story of the underdogs, folks who have been rejected but just wanted to be treated with respect and their identity accepted by everyone. They do not want your money or house, I think we as a community need emotional support rather than financial support. It is empowering to know that you can express yourself and show to world your true identity.

I guess sometimes I get emotional when I am saying some of the stuff, there are certain sensitive stuff which are triggers for me when I start to talk about things I might go out of context and get emotional.

Although most of my life I have not displayed many emotions all my life a lot of folks complain that I don't display emotions at all they tend to think that I am an emotionless guy but unfortunately, this is not the truth.

I do have emotions and they are very complex I am not great at displaying emotions which is quite evident but that doesn't mean that I am an emotionless guy, it is just I am not good at expressing emotions. I guess I am not the only man who suffers from this complex, I have seen other men struggle and I certainly don't feel proud of that.

Anyway coming back to the pride parade, I think for me it offers hope and makes new connections. I don't know what it could mean but as a bisexual man, I need to connect with those folks who can see me for what I am.

Often I am tired of hiding and running away, I want to show my true self to everyone and tell everyone what I am but often I do not dare to say it. It is often exhausting and suffocating, it just hampers my mental health but then again I will have to live like this for the rest of my life.

Often I feel I am leading a double life and that I would have to protect my secret at all costs as if my life would be dependent on it. If by any chance the secret is revealed then I fear there could be some consequences which I am not ready to face.

I know that a lot of us are leading a double life and I am sure there must be a lot of folks who are feeling frustrated and are tired of this and I can understand how they must be feeling. From the outside, they might look heterosexual that is because they are scared for their life and do not want to jeopardise it.

I know this sounds crazy sometimes but in a country like ours there are a lot of people who just marry someone under the pressure of maintaining the secret and I cannot imagine the kind of horror they might have to go through just because they cannot spill it out.

I can only imagine what it feels like to be them, I mean it is almost like you are forced to sleep with that person who you don't even like and are not even attracted to by a long distance. It might feel like you are doing a horrible thing you might even feel like your life has been wasted by not being vocal enough.

Then there is your partner who might have very high hopes for you after all marriage is a very big thing and most folks get married only once in their lifetime so for the other person marriage is a big thing and if he finds out their partner might be a homosexual it is hard to imagine what it would be like.

I mean they might not know what you really are but eventually, as the marriage progresses you get to know each other better inside and out. The opposite person will find out the truth and once the truth is out it is hard to tell which way the things would go.

You could be shamed by your own family or your family would disown you or you might be alienated by everyone. In such cases how is an individual supposed to survive, I can't think of a way that a certain individual can come out of it so easily.

It could be so hard for anyone to deal with such a situation not to mention the alienation could hamper your self-confidence and the kind of impact it has on mental health. The individual might be facing anxiety problems or even go into depression.

We never know what could happen, I think it is a time-ticking bomb the more you try to hide the secret the harder will it be to let it remain a secret and eventually the truth will come out I guess and there is no anecdote for it.

In a way, we are all fucked up I often ask myself the same question how long will I be able to hide the truth for now we think that by not revealing it we are safe but we cannot do it indefinitely. The truth will come out in one way or the other, people who lie often get exposed in one way or the other. You can fool them but for how long and then ultimately it is up to the people who are around you how they process the information.

If you are one of the folks who are accepted for your sexuality and your family would support you in all your decisions then I think it's great to be a part of that family which does that. I think there are really few families in India who accept you if you come out of the closet and declare your sexuality and if by chance you are like me then you are royally fucked my friend, I don't think you can do much you can try to run away but I don't think it works practically.

You could run away from them and move to a new city and eventually, you would find folks who are like those whom you were running from or you could find people who are worse than the folks who you were running away from. It doesn't matter where you go eventually you will find people who hate LGBT and living a life like this could be a hell hole for you.

My number one problem with this disclosing thing is the kind of reactions you get, it becomes hard for anyone to come out. If you people around you are very supportive then yes it becomes easy for you and you might feel comfortable coming out of the closet but that is not the case always.

If you are in an environment which is not very supportive of such things then things can get complicated, and you start to have second thoughts about whether or not you can tell them and if you tell them how they are going to react.

That has been my fundamental question since the ages and after a certain age if you don't get romantically involved then folks would want you to get married as they feel you won't be able to find a partner after a certain age and the more you grow older the harder it would get to hide your secret and eventually you might have to just give up and tell the truth.

What happens after telling the truth is again very subjective I would not recommend everyone to do it. If you are in such a situation that you can reveal then yes go ahead and do it but if there is a doubt in your mind please be careful as these are very thin lines and anything you could do can have dangerous consequences.

I know I was supposed to talk about pride parades in this chapter but I had to give some background on certain stuff before I could make my point. Although I think I have made my point clear in starting of this chapter, it is such sensitive that I wanted to stress more on this stuff as I hear a lot of stories and rumors on the internet.

I feel like anyone who is part of this LGBT community is like a part of my family even though I might not know. I feel like there is a connection; we share certain things, mostly tragedy and sadness, and I don't want any of them to feel lonely.

I have made some mistakes in the past and I hope that others can learn from my mistakes and they don't repeat the same ones which I did which is why I don't think anyone should take this pride parade lightly.

Some folks feel that we are doing something evil and immoral and we are going to corrupt others as well with our pride parades. This is one criticism which we constantly get from the other side and I don't think that's true.

This parade is no different from thousands of marches that happen every year which happen to educate people on different issues. After all these marches or parades are there to educate people and in a way inspire people and let them know that they are not online in this world and they can reach for help if needed.

It could be awareness of heart risk, mental health, human rights etc. There are tons of things that have rallied some people to join them while others share their videos, there could be a debate on certain things but no one says that you have an evil agenda behind your rallies and that you want everyone to become like you.

If someone is calling a rally for cancer, it means that they want you to know that it is important that people get tested for cancer as they might have a chance to detect it early and you might focus on the treatment if it gets detected early.

That is the main intention behind all this rallying for cancer and discussing different types of cancers and their symptoms. They are not here to make you feel that everyone has cancer so if you are gonna take it the wrong way we all will be affected by some or the other type of cancer is just crazy and it is so untrue.

Just like those rallying for a certain cause want to educate and accept the reality, the main focus of the pride parade is not to force everyone to become homosexual or bisexual. I think whoever thought of this is kind of crazy.

The idea that we want all the kids to become like us is just out of this world and why would any gay, lesbian, bisexual, or transgender person want everyone to be just like them? I don't think any in the wildest dreams would want that to happen.

It's just a crazy theory just to suppress someone or something they don't like or hate. They just can't stand the sight that so many people, those people whom they view as weird and mentally unfit to live in a society are gathering as a group and telling the rest of the world what they are.

The bottom line is they don't like seeing us which is the reason they come up with new excuses, they don't have a problem with other rallies where they talk about rights and issues that deal with people from different sections of society and they would not even fight about it or talk about it.

For them, it is a non-existing issue but when it comes to the LGBT community they are like no we cannot allow it to happen as it is unnatural and against the concept of our religion and god and it is laughable that allowing a bunch of people who are raising some flags are slogans can endanger so many people.

I am really at the loss of words, I don't like this attitude for them it might be a horrible thing but for a lot of us, I think it could be a great way to tell our story to the world. It is a way to get accepted by new people find new friends and new relationships lead a great life and be happy for a change.

VI

Myths

I think there are a lot of myths when it comes to the LGBT community. They must be addressed because they confuse many people. There is so much propaganda regarding homosexuals, bisexuals and transgender.

The biggest problem with these myths is that they not only create confusion but they also allow us to create a stereotype which is bad for us. Getting stereotyped is the last thing we would require because getting stereotyped means that we are allowing other people to put us in one box.

It could have a serious impact on us, it can even dehumanize us in such a way that our deaths may be celebrated. I know these are not nice things to say but someone would have to say it as it is a very serious matter.

Maybe I am not the first person to address these things but often we neglect this kind of topic because this is not a top priority for us. I think we should make it a top priority for a lot of folks because the kinds of myths that are being propagated to folks who may not even have an opinion are disgusting.

We have to be very careful when we are talking about these kinds of subjects as they could cause a lot of damage, especially when we see so many kids who are confused about sexuality.

At this time we should try to focus on our narratives and try to help each other out as I see a lot of moral policing nowadays. Some folks on the internet have no regrets about killing us and they take pride in beating us and forcing us to become somebody other than what we truly are.

I mean it is appalling to see people giving us open death threats on public platforms and nothing happens to their accounts. Their accounts continue to operate whereas our accounts are cyberbullied every day.

Every day we are told the kind of filth we are and how we don't have a right to live and we get horrible DMs every day. It must be so hard for anyone to deal with this kind of trauma just because their sexuality is different from others.

Despite repeated times these people's accounts are reported nothing much happens and we have only option is to block the account but sometimes that is not enough. There have been situations where people are forced to either delete their accounts or lock their accounts.

I don't think in a civilized world such as ourselves we should allow cyberbullying. We have often raised our voices against bullying and how it affects our mental health but we don't do anything against cyberbullying because for us it is a small matter.

I don't think it is a small matter it is a huge matter, it could hamper a lot of people's self-esteem, worth and mental health. Mental health is really important because people might often go into depression or might get anxiety-related disorders.

I know this may sound far stretched but the nasty comments one makes online which are hurtful to others can cause a lot of damage and pain. People will have a tough time doing their day-to-day activities because it has caused trauma for them.

We never know how a certain person reacts to such mean comments, not only do they make mean comments they also send rape and death threats. It is really hard to imagine what one has to go through if they hear such things in their DMs.

I think it is absurd that so many of them are getting abused but nothing happens to the aggressors. I don't know how rape threats can be allowed on public platforms and those guys who made such comments usually apologize and get away with it.

You say such nasty things about a person and abuse someone in their DM's and after all the trauma they had to go through because of such comments, they think that one apology is going to solve the problem.

I don't think this is the solution who is going to be responsible if something happens to that person will they take the responsibility I don't think they can. Instead, they will try to be over-smart and will try to play the victim card.

I don't know how can someone play the victim when they have been over-aggressive and destroyed a person inside and outside in such a horrible manner and when those jokes hurt you they come up with stuff like "it is just a joke", or "it is not real".

I don't think these are jokes and I certainly do not think that they can get away with jokes. How on earth can you claim to make jokes when you threaten to rape someone? I don't think threatening can be ever considered a joke.

Anyone who thinks that these are jokes needs to be punished with the harshest punishment. I don't understand how these things are being allowed. Even after giving screenshots and references the situation is such that they get away quite easily.

It is frustrating to see that this kind of behaviour is displayed by a lot of people on the internet and they can get away with it in the name of freedom of speech, and anonymity which is absurd. You cannot get away just because you are anonymous, I think it is high time these accounts are tracked and they need to be booked and have to know the consequence of such actions.

They think they can get away with threats online but I think if we want we can take action against these accounts the biggest problem is that there are so many accounts. It is really hard to take action against all of them, you can't put them all in jail and even if we can put them in jail the case would be quashed very soon. So we cannot do much about it but I think we should ponder about how to tackle such people online.

Anyways coming back to the myths regarding our community, one of the biggest myths plaguing our community is the fact that we all are the same. We are not the same people, a homosexual person is different from a bisexual person and a homosexual, or bisexual is different from transgender and so on.

Each sexuality is different, homosexual means someone who is attracted to the same gender whereas bisexual means a person who is attracted to both genders. Transgender on the other hand is completely different, it means that the person feels like he is from a different gender than what they were assigned at birth.

Not only our sexualities are different but our personalities are different, it is not as if all the gays and lesbians would behave in the same way. Just like all heterosexuals are different and unique, we are also different no matter what our sexualities might be.

Everyone in the community is not sex sex-hungry maniac it is contrary to what most people might think. Most of us want a normal intimate relationship with the opposite person who can understand us and can have long-term relationships with that person.

At the end of the day, we are humans and we need to be loved and cherished by the other person. It feels good to be vulnerable in the arms of another person and just like other humans, we would like to be validated which I believe is the most human trait.

I am not saying that everyone would be like me but there are a lot of people like me who would love to have a great partner who can understand us and not judge us because frankly, it is very easy to judge.

Anyone can pass a random judgment on anyone, everything is all white and black when you look at it from the outside but if you take a moment and put yourself in our situation and then try to see the world through our eyes then you will have a newer perspective and perhaps you might not even hate us.

Yes, there might be some folks who are looking for short-term relationships and are not looking for commitment and I don't find anything wrong in it. A lot of heterosexuals indulge in that kind of practice and at some level, I can understand why someone would choose a short-term relationship over a long-term relationship.

Long-term relationships can be quite scary and we never know who can hurt us in the worst possible way so we do not want to go all in some people don't go for long-term relationships they do not want to get emotionally hurt and are very scared and as I said there is nothing wrong in it but to assume that everyone from this community is like this is far stretched lie and it is not good for us as a community if a large population believe those lies about us.

Another big myth which is propagated against us is that we are cunning people who deceive to get whatever we want. A lot of people would not believe this but there are a lot of people who believe in these things.

They think that all we do is pretend that we are not homosexual or bisexual and in reality, we do not have such feelings because they do not exist. But I would like to tell them how wrong they are in thinking we fake this kind of thing.

First of all, if you feel that all LGBT people are full of liars who would do anything they want then you are plain wrong. We are not manipulative people who would fake emotions and arm-twist things just to suit our agenda.

I think you will find good-hearted and nice people who you can hang out with just like the rest of the other people. The biggest problem with a lot of folks is that they see through their lens and once you know someone is gay and now everything is wrong with that person.

Instead of judging him based on whether or not he is a nice person they start to judge them based on their sexuality and assume that everything they do must be wrong or they is a very horrible person.

A person's sexuality cannot decide whether or not he is a nice person or not. I think there are various methods you can determine whether or not from your perspective a person is good or not.

Firstly you would have to see the kind of ideologies they subscribe to, the ideas they believe in and then you have to see how that person reacts when someone is being mean and lastly, the kind of things they do once they have supreme power over the other person or a community.

I think according to me these are the things that are required minimum before you can declare someone that they are a good or bad person. I find it weird that people can pass this kind of judgment in a matter of few minutes.

Often in life, we may think that we know someone but something terrible happens and we are in shock and disbelief that all our life we felt like we knew someone and then this truth bomb happens and you start to feel you never knew this person. I know this mere imagination makes it look like it is very crazy but sometimes I guess it is more of a feeling rather than knowing.

So if you are one of those people who hate us for our sexuality and if by reading this you can change your view on certain things then I think I would feel that I would have succeeded because at times I feel like we don't talk and discuss stuff and at times talking and discussing would solve a lot of problems.

I know a lot of folks would get angry just for trying to suggest a dialogue with those who hate us and probably want to kill us but I still think there could be a common ground. We always think that they are our enemies but I think that is not always the case.

I have been monitoring some activism and movements throughout the world. I have noticed that these activists who want to spread the idea or ideology want to debate. They just love to talk and interact with more people.

According to them the more they engage the better will be for their activism and obviously, I will not be able to name the field and the kind of activism they do because some of it is very sensitive things right now I might offend a lot of people if I name them.

Anyways, the style and approach they have is quite simple. Don't hate the people who strongly believe in it is the number one rule, your fight is against an idea and the society which propagates those ideas and not against the people.

They are victims just like you because they have fallen for the propaganda. If we look into it from a psychological perspective then hatred of an individual or a community comes from fear and fear could be logical or illogical.

I know some of the things that I am saying are not easily understood but sometimes we have to look at it from a third-person perspective rather than always looking from a first-person or second-person perspective. I firmly believe that the problem we have is a very complex one and we would require a lot of help to solve this.

At the end of the day, they call us zombies and we must note down each of the terminology that they give us and try to analyze it in a non-emotional way and try to understand the kind of people we are dealing with.

I inclined toward psychology since I was a kid because I was always fascinated by the human brain and human behaviour. I think we must try to understand the people who don't like us or hate us. Yes if someone crosses the line we should take action against them but some people have not crossed the line.

It is our duty that we have to educate in whatever we can so that they can support us or even if they cannot support us, they can at least appreciate our point of view and understand the fact that we are not here to harm anyone and we just want to live our life peacefully and we do not want our personal lives to be intruded by random folks.

No one likes it when their personal life is being invaded by a random person or a person who might know them and it feels like someone is choking you to death. Just like how you feel disgusted when someone tries to be smart and make things public which they do not have the right to do so.

No matter how close you are person you do not have the right to share the details which involves another person because you have not taken any consent and since they have not given the consent you might be leaking some private information which might jeopardise a lot of things.

For example, screenshots of whom you are chatting with or any video or audio proof of conversations, photos, or videos that are not there on the internet. If you are doing this for your gain or whatever fucked up the reason you chose to be like this you are a complete asshole.

I am sorry for the use of this language but I guess I do not know how to describe my feelings sometimes I become emotional and I think I must write what I feel rather than being diplomatic about it.

I cannot respect that kind of person who engages in this kind of behaviour and leaks sensitive information about people. Frankly, I feel frustrated but I guess I don't think we can do much about it after all it is not a big crime.

Moving on, the major point I am trying to make is that the privacy of an individual matters more than any community morality. We all have our morality and it doesn't matter what we believe unless we are using it to harm others.

I strongly believe that in the 21st century, different people can have different ideas and visions and we need not accept all belief systems and ideologies. But some people, don't care for all these things all they care about is doing moral policing.

They want to impose their ideas on us and that is why they like to call us zombies because, in reality, those folks are the real zombies who are afraid of truth and reality. They don't like seeing people of different thinking and ideology.

All their life they have been in their bubble and if they see anyone out of that bubble they go crazy and they start to behave like zombies. Zombies by definition are the dead people who have been raised to do only 1 thing and that 1 thing will be decided by whoever controls them.

Now I do not know who controls them and what they want the point I am trying to make is that they do not have the thinking ability, they are doing whatever they are being told. Just like those zombies, we have folks who are human versions of zombies and they don't care for analytical and logical reasoning.

All they care for is the mission that they have been assigned, they don't care if someone gets hurt, and they do not care if something bad happens all they care about is to do exactly what they have been hearing since childhood and that is people from LGBT community are bad people and something needs to be done to either eradicate people associate or eradicate the entire idea.

I think we need to be wary of those people or zombies because they are dangerous and they don't have an open mind. The problem with these zombies is that they don't have their brains and do whatever some other person tells them to do.

They call us zombies but in reality, they are the actual zombies who have no sense of thinking and they brandish such things to others while it shows reflection of themselves. The most idiotic thing in all of this is the fact that they get so much support.

There is no hope for these people, all they do is harass people who are not like them. It saddens me the kind of power these ignorant people possess and the kind of damage they can do from their actions.

Yes, I think the stuff they do to us can harm us in both ways ie., physically and emotionally and you might be left scarred for life. We must talk about the trauma and the kind of impact these ignorant people have on us.

It is not fair the kind of harassment and bullying one has to face due to their sexuality, it almost feels like a crime even though it has been decriminalised. I don't know how long we all will be feeling like this and is there any solution for these kinds of things?

I believe that there is nothing I can do at this point other than the fact that I am constantly ranting I am about and it might be irritating to a lot of folks who might be reading this and wondering why I am doing this.

My main motive is to make people realize how horrible they have been and especially how some people can be very violent and cause so much pain for a crime which we didn't even commit. I think it has affected me both physically and mentally which is the reason I am using those words to express my feelings.

Some of the words which I have written may not make sense to some people or a lot of people but they make sense to me if you look at things from my perspective. From my perspective, I just don't like certain things I see in my day-to-day life on the internet and in the real world.

I think it makes sense from my point of view, sometimes I feel very powerless and frankly, I don't know what to do. I guess there are a lot of folks who feel like they are powerless and they don't know what on earth to do. I don't think I am the only one who feels like if I am wrong and other folks won't feel like this then I would be happy.

But if there are people who feel like me then that means that they can relate to me which is the whole point. I write stuff which makes absolutely no sense and which can relate to other people and I think I am usually on the point.

Anyway, I think I have gone a little bit off-topic but that is alright I guess, occasionally we all should be given a pass for a little bit of ranting. Hopefully, anyone reading this can bear and tolerate me and hopefully, despite all my rants I can tell some interesting stories and make my readers think.

I think one big myth we need to talk about gay men loves to dress like women which is completely untrue. Some men love to dress like women but they are called transsexual people and they have nothing to do with being gay.

A gay man is a person who is attracted to another man, although gay is an umbrella term for both gays and lesbians. Gay means homosexuals ie., attracted to the same gender and it has nothing to do with dressing up like women.

There are a lot of cross-dressers who do this for professional purposes but they are not gay and unlike most of the gay celebrities I have seen, none of them likes to dress up like a woman. They are men who behave just like another heterosexual men.

They behave like other men and the only difference is in their sexuality your heterosexual man is attracted to females whereas your homosexual man is attracted to other males. They might be attracted to heterosexual or homosexual men.

Now obviously there will be a conflict of interest when a homosexual man feels attracted towards a heterosexual male because the other person will not have the same feelings after all, their sexuality is quite different.

Just like not all gay men love to dress up like women and not all lesbians love to dress up like a man. I know this is a very idiotic stereotype that exists and a myth which is propagated everywhere, yes there might be some women who like to dress up like a man but that does not mean that everyone would be like that.

I think dressing up like a man or a woman is dependent on that particular person and it might not be the same for everyone. Some people like to do it, and some people hate doing that such as dressing up as a person of the opposite gender and I don't think we should judge anyone based on that.

Everyone has their reason for behaving in such a manner and we cannot stereotype that a certain sexuality or race acts in this way because we are not robots we are humans. We should not suppose that everyone belonging to a particular community behaves in this way only, I think this kind of stereotyping needs to stop as it can cause a lot of mental stress.

It might not be a mental stress for you but for the opposite person when they hear certain stereotypes they feel like someone has trapped them and they cannot get out of that box forever. I think a lot of people are ignorant of a lot of things and they might stereotype a lot of things.

For me, stereotyping starts with generalizing anything and generalizing is not a good thing because we are not open to the idea that a particular person from a particular community can do a particular kind of activity.

It is like we have put labels on everything, causing harm rather than good. Putting labels on people can cause disappointment because if they happen to do a certain thing which we don't expect then it can cause a lot of damage to the brain.

Now suddenly all my life I was addicted to some kind of lifestyle with a particular style of thinking I have to rethink all ideologies and whether or not the ideas and belief systems I believe in are true or not.

My stereotype has been broken because I had put limitations on a certain individual who would not be able to do this because of this reason but suddenly they have done something extraordinary.

It was so extraordinary that I had to rethink my belief system which led to stereotyping a particular person has eventually made me doubt my belief system. A belief system for a particular person is very close to heart when their belief system is challenged they act weirdly.

They get agitated and refuse to believe what is in front of them because it is like proving to a very religious person that the religion they follow is not a divine thing but a man-made thing. It would drive them crazy initially and that person would call you all kinds of names.

What happens after their belief system is challenged can be divided into 2 categories because I believe there are 2 kinds of people on this planet and whenever our belief system is shaken to the core we behave differently.

The first group are those people who are angry at first but eventually would understand the point you are making because even though they might be angry initially since they have an open mind they would think about it and try to rationalize it and try to come to a logical conclusion.

The second group are those people who would never accept it but instead will keep making illogical comparisons which makes no sense because they have an empty mind. They are not open to everything, they fear that they will become someone else and they would hate themselves.

So the only way to stop is to make other people look stupid or irrelevant and say stuff that does not make sense because they have to prove wrong they are right and everyone else is wrong and in the quest of proving wrong they start to do crazy stuff.

The homophobes are the second category of people because in their hearts deep down they know the reality but they refuse to acknowledge it. The day they start acknowledging us it would mean that all the time the fear-mongering that they did was wrong and they don't like it.

They do that one thing which makes us look bad in front of others, they accuse us of doing things which we have not indulged in, it is a standard gaslighting technique that has been used for centuries.

If you want to discredit someone and make sure that no one takes that person seriously then all you have to do is throw crazy allegations at them and they will go in defensive mode and once they go in the defensive mode you dictate the terms of that argument.

Eventually, the other person loses credibility and once I lose credibility whatever I say is wrong and inaccurate because I have been put in a defensive situation because I said or did something which is not morally acceptable.

Now the entire argument becomes personal, and all the contents of the argument go into the garbage bin because now my character has been assassinated and now I have officially lost the argument and since I am a bad person whatever I do should be considered as a bad thing.

So if Dan is a bad person and he is bisexual then that means that all bisexuals are bad people and the kind of stuff bisexuals engage in is also very bad stuff. Now since I am representing the LGBT community I have been proved by nobody that I am bad and the LGBT community I represent is also bad.

So these homophobes will conclude that all the people from the LGBT community are bad people who indulge in things which are considered morally wrong because one person from that community was proven wrong by their moral standards in front of a lot of people.

Well once you have successfully pulled out this trick, you can get anyone in defensive position and it is a well-known trick that has been used by a lot of people to get whatever they want and they exploit the opposite person using this trick.

A lot of people I have come across in my life have used this trick for a different purpose to justify a lot of horrible things sometimes to get their own needs met or it could be some other reason which we might not be aware of. I think at the end of the day we need to be wary of these kinds of people because they are everywhere.

These people not only confuse us but they also confuse people around and they trick others into hating us and making them feel like this is the only right thing to do. I don't have a solution but I think if we can expose their tricks and tactics to the opposite person then surely we can avoid this because no one likes being gaslighted.

It is one of the worst feelings you would get, at the moment it might not feel like you have been gaslighted but eventually you would feel that someone has played psychological tricks on you and they have won and you can't do anything about it.

VII
Gays and Lesbians

OK, let's talk about gays and lesbians in this chapter, although we have talked about them throughout this boo,k I will focus specifically on both sexualities as there is so much we can discuss about them.

Let's discuss gays, as there are a lot of things to discuss about them. As I told you earlier, gay is an umbrella term that means homosexual. It could mean a man who is attracted to another man. Gay could also refer to a lesbian, which means a female who is attracted to another female.

As per the Government of India, we have 2.5 million gays and lesbians based on self-declaration by 2012, which is like 12 years ago, and if we go by activists' numbers, then the total number is around 125 million people, which I think is a huge number.

I think it is important that we discuss this number because I never knew that there were so many people who were out in the open who had disclosed their sexuality. For me, this number is huge and surprising.

These are the number of people who have declared themselves as gay or lesbian, imagine the number of people who have chosen not to declare it and are living a secret life. If we add those numbers, I can only see the numbers that are a very sizeable proportion, even if we compare them against a population of 1.4 billion.

Even if we count the number of people who have come out, it is a very good number. I used to think that we could not do anything because our numbers were very small, but that is not the scenario today.

Our population is more than that of any religious minority, although we cannot compare our situation with any religious minority people with a much lesser population have stood up as a community and demanded their rights and taken what is rightfully theirs.

We don't want to be treated specially, just like other heterosexual people have rights which have been granted by the constitution we just want those rights to be granted to us so that we can live a peaceful life and no tom dick and Harry should intervene in our life.

I don't think that is asking too much what we are asking is already in effect for other people it is just as people from different sexualities we want those things to be implemented to us because everyone deserves an equal chance no matter our gender and sexualities we should all be treated equally in front of the law.

I mean, we are not asking for a reservation or special rights to be included, just some amendments so that there are no moral and social obligations when it comes to living in India as part of this community.

Despite all the fights and movements in India regarding LGBT, I think a lot of people don't feel safe. A lot of experts and critics argue that we are a discriminated group throughout the country. The law speaks of a different situation, whereas society tells a different story.

The ground reality is quite different from the law, yes, according to the law, we have rights and we can do this and that, but how many landlords sell a particular house to a person belonging to the LGBT community?

As soon as they find out about your sexuality, their body language and behaviour change completely as if they are talking to a criminal, and sometimes we are treated worse than criminals. It is a shame that very few societies rent out or sell to gays and lesbians.

It is clear discrimination on their part, and it shows that despite all the efforts, the change on the ground is very far, and no matter how many laws or regulations we might have, we still have a long way to go before acceptance becomes a part of our society.

Unfortunately, in our societies, there are many taboos, and being gay or lesbian is one of them. When it comes to dealing with the taboo, we have a standard way of dealing with it. Here are the following steps that we generally follow when we deal with such things.

The first step is to deny that such a thing exists, and when they don't listen, ask them to give the proof, and when they start to give you the proof, they discard it, saying that they are mentally ill and no normal or sane person would indulge in such behaviour.

When the proof is clear, they start saying stuff that does not make sense and start attacking that community or making personal remarks. At this stage, they are well aware that they do not have anything to say appropriately.

Anyway, I think a lot of people use the same method while arguing, and since no one has objected till now, they seem to get away with it. They use similar logic while debating other stuff, which they feel is not normal and is unwarranted.

I think a couple of mainstream celebrities have come out as gay, although their acceptance might be low, still I think it is good that their family have accepted them. Even if the other folks who follow the entertainment industry might not have accepted him.

As far as lesbians are concerned, so far there is only 1 athlete, I think, who has openly come out as lesbian, and in the entertainment industry in India, I have not heard about any celebrity who is openly a lesbian, although there are movies with lesbian depictions in recent times. I think there might be quite a few lesbians who might be afraid to come out because they do not want to jeopardise their lives.

I don't have the official number when it comes to lesbians because whatever the data is, it is classified into whether or not you identify as homosexual, heterosexual, or bisexual. As per the report, there is 17% of the population who identify as homosexual, that is, either gay or lesbian.

0.9% of the population identifies as bisexual, so if we combine the data of both homosexual and bisexual populations in India, then we have 2.6% of the population. This data is very old, more than a decade ago, so this number should certainly be more than what it was a decade ago.

So, y if we look at numbers, then yes, we have a significant number, but then again, you would have to look at the other side. The other side is not so great, I mean on one side, we talk about how our numbers are increasing and more people are becoming part of our community, and on the other hand, we are still afraid that we are still discussing stuff like we are living in the Stone Age.

I think there is a huge difference between what is written on the paper called the Constitution and what is being practised on the ground, and that is the reason, despite having so many laws and stuff and having so many numbers, there is fear among the individuals.

A lot of people who speak on this issue are heterosexual folks. I used to think that all the people who speak on this issue are people belonging to our community, but now I am starting to realise why this happens.

I used to think that this fear was limited to me, but this is not the reality; there are a lot of folks who have the same fear as me. Probably that is the reason you do not see them a lot doing activism, because eventually, you become a target.

I know this is going to make a lot of people angry, but I see very few lesbians in the mainstream media. I don't even see a lot of lesbians on social media. I see a lot of gays but very few lesbians. I don't know what is the actual reason behind this.

Online, I have been able to connect with other gay and bisexual men, but I have not been able to come in contact with a lesbian, and often it feels like we are alienating them. If there are 1.7% homosexuals, then there should be a lot of lesbians around us.

I think maybe for a lot of women, it is tough to come out because they get judged more than men, and they are told to have a higher sense of emotionality, rationality, and responsibility compared to men.

So things are very complicated when it comes to lesbians, as it is not always possible to spot a lesbian. I think it would be very rude to say that I can spot a lesbian just by looking at her. I have tried out some of the sites and looked at some of the profiles of some lesbians, although none of them belonged to India.

I have tried searching on Quora, and   I have seen a few profiles, but it is hard to tell whether or not they are real because on the internet, you see a lot of fake profiles, especially a lot of female accounts that seem to be run by men to gain popularity.

I believe the term is called catfish accounts, where they post random pictures they can get online so that they can get a lot of likes and followers. A lot of accounts with thousands of followers turn out to be catfish accounts.

Of course, these accounts get exposed when somebody sheds light on their accounts and tells the real story behind these accounts, and once the culprit is exposed, I guess the account loses followers and eventually no respect for the person who had committed such fraud.

If I am not mistaken, a lot of lesbians might encounter someone online who pretends to be a lesbian, but it turns out that the account is run by a man because they just want to find someone online, and since they find no one and are very desperate, they use this method.

Anyone would assume that is a very pathetic thing to do, yes, you are right,t but there might be folks I don't know if this has happened to anyone but I think this might have happened because there have been incidents in the past where some female accounts were found to be run by men.

It is a very big possibility that some men, mostly heterosexual ones, would try to create a fake woman profile who is a lesbian with a fake photo online, and try to flirt and get pictures and videos online. I don't know the legality of such things because usually, people get away with such stuff because there are so many fake accounts.

Until and unless they are spreading false information about you, sharing some pictures without your prior approval, or cyberbullying someone to the extent that they do something extreme, you cannot take action. Even if they had indulged in some of the other things that have been stated above, I don't think action will be taken. Our law is unique when it comes to these kinds of crimes.

Although we have rules and regulations specified in our constitution, if it is implemented properly, then we can put a lot of people in jail, but the problem is that we would have so many people in jail, and with our jails already so overcrowded. I don't think our judiciary would take such accounts seriously, and they usually let these kinds of people go with some kind of warning.

Once they are scot-free, they will probably target some other person. This time, they might take extra precautions so they don't get caught, and life goes on for them, and it should go on for us as well. I don't think there is much we can do; maybe we just need to be careful while we are online and understand the risks of being online.

I guess we cannot do much when it comes to these things, but if these things do happen, then I would be interested to know what action a particular individual has taken against these accounts, and if it has never happened in your life, then I guess you have nice people around you.

I am pretty much sure that this kind of stuff has happened to at least a few of them, I do not have the proof but there is this gut feeling I have from the inside which keeps telling me that somewhere I am right because if I am not right this will make me look like a stupid person.

I think many girls and women are close to their fathers because there is a very big stereotype that says fathers are more likely to be protective towards their daughters and mothers towards their sons.

So, if we go by this logic, most women should feel safe with their father in telling their secrets, so if someone wants to come out as lesbian, then she should be telling her father. Still, it is not so easy for her because not many fathers would be supportive of this decision.

A lot of fathers are overprotective of their daughters, and even if they find out she has a boyfriend, they get agitated and go out of their way to protect their daughters. Generally, a lot of them would disapprove of such a relationship if they found out their daughter is in love with someone.

I think it has a lot more to do with their reputation than the choice of the daughter, because in India, reputation is everything, and you have to protect it at all costs. This is the situation if the daughter is involved in a heterosexual relationship, and the possibilities are endless on how things might unfold.

Now, imagine if she is in a homosexual relationship, the kind of knee-jerk reaction that is going to be displayed by their father is unimaginable. I think very few women are comfortable sharing this piece of information with their fathers about their sexuality.

If a woman knows her father very well, then the chances are she can take the risk of telling it to her father, and how the father reacts well is a separate issue altogether because the first step is to convince yourself that you can tell your father without any major consequences.

So if she can convince herself that she can proudly tell to her father, then you can proceed to the next step and then see your father's reaction to your confession but there is a high possibility you cannot tell your father because you are convinced he is going to behave most negatively to this news.

If you can tell the father and he accepts you, then I would say that is great, you should be glad that you have such a lovely and understanding family, which most people do not have. In case you happen to tell your father and he still reacts negatively, then you have messed up, and we don't know what the consequences are going to be.

He could physically beat you, get you married to someone against your wishes, or even lock you in the house forever. The results are endless, and each one is as horrific as the next one. If you choose not to reveal this secret, then you will have to go to the next step, which is telling your mother.

Often, I note some competition between mother and daughter to prove their worth. So there is always some tension when it comes to this relationship. Now your brain is convinced that going to your father is a horrible decision, now you have to tell your mother.

If by any chance you are somewhat close to your mother, you do tell her your secret, and she understands and supports you, then there will be a huge task at hand. How do you convey this message to your father and the rest of the family?

I think there is a possibility that you tell your secret to your mother, and she goes and tells the same thing to your father,r and eventually they try to convince you to get married, and by marrying someone, you would not be getting these kinds of thoughts.

This is one thing they constantly keep doing if, for some reason, they know about your sexuality. They would treat it as if it were a mental illness, and you need to stop having such thoughts, and they would suggest remedies so that you do not get those kinds of thoughts.

They will call you brainwashed and will ask you the name of the person who is influencing you to do all these kinds of things. They would not listen to you when you told them that nothing of the sort is there.

They would make you feel that the feelings you have for the same gender are not real, and the only reason you are having such thoughts is because you do not have a man in your life. They would select some matches for you and would like to select one of them so that you get settled in your life and stop having such thoughts.

Now the next step is trying to explain to your relatives and your mother that you are not suffering from any disease, what you feel is completely normal, and that your sexuality is just as real as any heterosexual person.

You don't feel attracted to a person of the opposite gender, and like someone of your gender. If your relationship blooms with that special one, then you might think of settling down, and now ,at this point, your family will realise that it is probably too late and your mind can't be changed.

At this point, you are royally fucked I guess and it is so complicated that most of them run away from their families because sometimes it is just too much to handle. In another situation, you don't tell your family about your sexuality, and they might want to get you married.

In an ideal scenario, you should have resisted, but then again, you are too afraid to tell because of the consequences, and you give up and marry the guy despite being a lesbian, which complicates your life even further.

Even if you are a heterosexual woman, trying to make a marriage work with an unknown person is so tough, and now, on top of that, you have a special situation where a closeted lesbian is now married to a straight guy.

As I said earlier, marriage is a sacred thing for a lot of folks, and they would expect the girl to run the house and make babies. Now the real tragedy is no one knows the truth, and not just 1 life but 2 lives have been destroyed, and several more will be affected because of this decision.

That girl's life is destroyed as she is forced to make babies with a person she doesn't even like. Forget about the likes and dislikes, she would never be around that person of that gender because she doesn't feel attracted to or would want to get intimate if she were ever given a choice.

The second is the boy who had high hopes for his partner, he hoped that she would be a great wife to him and they would have a wonderful family. Together, he, his wife, and the kids in the future are going to be immediate family.

His life would be devastated when he would find out that he married a lesbian, he might get angry and pissed off at the girl and might even feel cheated. He might be right in a way, after all, it was not his fault; he did not force her to get married.

He was looking for a girl who would probably make him happy and become his life partner, and in return, all he got was disappointment. Certainly, we cannot blame the girl because she was afraid and she was just a mute spectator, and even if she did reveal her true sexuality, then she would have to face the worst consequences from her side.

Fear can make you do things you normally wouldn't, and in this case, it was pretty much evident from the start, but it has altered many lives in the process. If the boy finds out the truth, then it is going to be the end of the marriage and a very big embarrassment.

And if the boy does not find out the reality and she continues to pretend that she is straight and raises a family with that guy, then she will probably feel disgusted for the rest of her life. I don't think she would be able to look at herself in the mirror.

She would probably have some identity crisis because if I were a gay person and I was forced to make babies with a person whom I never liked or didn't even like the gender, I don't think I could live with myself.

As a gay person, I would feel like I have murdered my soul, as my life has been completely wasted just to portray myself as a nice, normal person. I think it is an oxymoron doing that thing to please others and now you are disgusted at yourselves I think that is fucked up.

I think I would have mental health issues because it is not easy for me to comprehend that I did something that I will not forget for the rest of my life, and I don't have anyone to blame for it.

I can't blame the person I married because they did not force me to get married, and I certainly can't blame myself because I was in a situation, and I was trying to normalise the situation, and instead I went against my sexuality to marry someone whom I would feel disgusted by.

In some cases, you can blame the parents, but a lot of times they are under pressure from their relatives, friends, etc, as they don't want their kids to be alienated by society. No one wants their kid to be alienated, as often things go bad and they don't want this to happen.

So now we have to blame society for being homophobic and not accepting the children's sexuality, and forcing them to act similarly, and if you don't act in that prescribed normal way, then there is something wrong with you. And if you are not normal, then you have some sort of disease;

if you are attracted to the same gender, then you have a problem.

They will tell you all kinds of unscientific things to do to make sure that you are child recovers from the disease called being gay, and it is indeed a very sad commentary on the state of affairs. Families of well-educated people behave in this way so that they do not have to face this kind of embarrassment.

Eventually, they will start some counselling to make sure that you are convinced that being gay is just a feeling, it is in your power, and you can make it go away. If there is some kind of family counselling going on, then you should be lucky because a lot of people are not that lucky.

Several folks get beaten by their parents or their loved ones because they feel some kind of ghost has attacked their child. So to save the kid they will beat the shit out of the kid until the kid dies or they feel that the kid is fully recovered from the disease and it has happened in a lot of cases and reading those stories just breaks my heart.

I guess that is a lesbian side story, but for gays, it is not better because the chance of a man being identified as gay is much higher than a lesbian. I think it is tough to say who has it worse, I mean, it is worse for both of them.

People expect men to get married after a certain although a woman is expected to get married after a certain age I think the main difference is that if a woman does not want to get married then people might not think of her sexuality as coming in the way but if a man does it then there are a lot of questions that can be raised.

I agree that it is tough for a lesbian and her life can be made hell, but someone who is a closeted gay person has it tough because the first question that pops into their head when you say no to marriage is that you might be gay.

I am not kidding, once you reach a certain age, and if your immediate family wants you to get married, but for some reason, you delay them and tell them that you do not want to get married, or you need some time, and eventually,y they keep pushing you to get married.

If you are close to your mother, she might even search for some brides for you to get married, and most of the time, you just cannot straight no to their face. You can delay them for a while, but if you say no to the,m it will be very weird.

At the end of the day, you could delay them for a few months, maybe a couple of years, but eventually, you would have to give in to their demand. Now you have only 2 ways: either get married and complicate your life, or tell them that you are gay and complicate your life again.

I think the results are going to be the same, as I have tried to explain that a lesbian marrying a heterosexual man is worse for both parties; similarly, a gay man marrying a heterosexual woman is going to be a disaster for both of them.

If the woman knows about the truth after the marriage then she is going to be pissed and she is going to tell her immediate family and that immediate family is going to tell your family and once that story reaches your family you are royally fucked.

Imagine if you confess before the marriage that you cannot get married because you are gay, now you would be saving a lot of lives, but there is this danger of how your family would take this, and you never knew how someone from your family might react.

I think a lot of people are afraid to come out to their families regarding their sexuality as they do not want to get judged or are not sure what to do at this point. I have been confused all my life, and at this point, I don't even know what to do with my secret.

Now and then, people from my immediate family want me to get married, and they bring up this topic, and I am really afraid to tell them the reality. I am bisexual, and I don't have a problem getting married to a woman, but I think it is important that I tell the opposite person what my sexuality is.

After getting married, the couple usually gets very intimate, and suddenly you don't have any secrets; after all, it is very hard to keep secrets from your wife. I would never want to deceive anyone in a way that, some years into the marriage, they feel cheated.

Trust in any relationship takes time, and relationships are like trees; whether they are your friends or romantic partners, it takes time for you to get to know them, and they have to get to know you and understand.

In romantic relationships, intimacy is a key thing, and it can only be achieved if you have full trust. If you don't have complete trust, then it will be very weird for the couple, and to get that trust, it takes months, maybe years, to fully understand one another.

Once you feel that you have gotten to know the opposite person, you feel confident that your relationship is really strong with that person, and then suddenly they get to know about something that they did not see coming.

That person is heartbroken and is feeling cheated, they are now going through several range of emotions, and I would never want that to happen, it would be hard for me to face the person if I had hurt a person in that way.

I already have trust issues in my personal life, so I know what it is to feel betrayed and cheated. I would never want someone to go through that kind of mental agony that I had to go through, and it was horrible, so I would never want someone so close to my heart to go through it.

I am an open book any can read me, if you ask me a direct question I would answer you directly so it becomes awkward if I am in a situation where I am breaking someone's heart and that is the primary reason I would like a full disclosure before actually marrying someone because you never know how they would react.

I think this resonates with a lot of folks, whether you are heterosexual or homosexual, everyone deserves a full disclosure and the right to know the truth. Just because, for the sake of some person or to protect someone, we cannot destroy the other person.

I am hopeful that we can create a society where we would not have to lie on this key decision, such as marriage, and we can tell the truth wholeheartedly, as telling lies and deceiving is not a good thing to do.

VIII

Bisexuals

We had an interesting discussion on gays and lesbians primarily and how their lives are affected or can be affected by a lot of things. I tried to explain it simply as how there might be consequences whether you take action and there might be consequences if you do not take action.

Either way, there will be things coming your way that you cannot avoid I guess life is all about taking risks and decisions but these kinds of decisions can affect you and the people around so you have to be careful and think probably hundreds of times before you can come to a decision and tell it to everyone.

Most of the time I try to tell a story or rather try to tell something through that story sometimes it might feel stretched but my intention is not to bore you or take conversation in the other direction but try to tell you and show you the larger picture.

I think most of the time I can guess the kind of criticism I can get or I might get because I know myself very well. Sometimes I might get emotional as well and might use foul language although this can be said without using foul language I think it is important that whoever reads this book should know and understand my feelings.

Often we read a book and whatever the author tries to write we try to imagine a certain scenario where this kind of incident might take place and based on what the author has given us we try to visualize it in our brain and then come to a certain conclusion.

I think I don't like it I just want it to be a monologue, I am sitting right in front of me and you are kind of listening to whatever I am saying and your brain is just converting the text to speech for that I think it is necessary that sometimes wherever I use some cuss words are mandatory.

Although the cuss words might not be mandatory they represent my inner frustration, just like when you watch a video you get a representation of their inner thoughts whenever you read whatever I have written you should be able to visualize me and then see through me what I have been telling you rather imagining in your head.

I know that sometimes I can go off-topic and you might be even wondering what the hell I am even reading and does this makes sense. Initially, it might not make sense but if you read it in a complete context it might make sense as I try to tell a story by connecting different dots.

Initially, all my dots seem unrelatable but if you can bear with me for a while and complete a few paragraphs of the chapter you might be able to see the message I was trying to say. I think I am a little bit of a non-linear writer who is generally not straightforward when it comes to telling my thoughts.

My non-linear way of telling things does sit well with a lot of people who are reading because the topic on which I have written things needs feedback and trust me this is not some marketing strategy or anything.

I just hope more and more people can read this and if people from my country especially can read this and tell me honestly what they think of this then I think it would be great. Maybe some of the things that I might have said were completely ignorant and if I have written those things then that would make me an idiot.

And for that reason, I need the feedback of the people, even if one person buys it and shares the pdf I would certainly not have a problem with that. As long as I am getting the correct feedback, there are lots of myths when it comes to the LGBT community and maybe I might have said something which I should not have and I think I should be open to queries and criticism.

It is okay if you didn't like what you read, you can probably abuse me and tell me the things where I am wrong and I would probably acknowledge it and try to make amendments and release the book again if that is possible.

As I had said in the beginning my main motive behind writing this book is to make sure that it reaches every corner of the world now I know that no one knows me and I am a nobody and I have limited resources but I think this book can reach a lot of folks and it might even change the minds of a few who refuse to believe our truth.

It might even reach those people who are lost and in need, they might be looking for some kind of help and although this is not therapy they might be glad that someone in some corner of the world just wrote a book about them and let them know that they are not lonely in this world.

Although I am not an expert when it comes to LGBT topics and neither I have a degree or Ph.D. and I certainly haven't done anything in psychology that I should be giving lectures to hundreds of people I think that I am qualified enough to talk on that subject. Sometimes your experience is just alone enough to talk on a certain subject without having any kind of degree.

Of course, some people know more than me but I think I represent an average bisexual guy who is confused about a lot of things and if a certain average person comes out and tells his side of the story this might be a booster for a lot of people. This may or may not inspire a change or revolution but at least people start talking about it and hopefully, it can change a few hearts who currently don't approve of LGBT people.

I am a bisexual man and I feel attracted to both genders which might be a rare thing to hear for a lot of people because they might have heard of gays and lesbians but they might not be aware of what bisexual means.

A lot of people haven't processed the terms gay and lesbian and they might have so many doubts regarding gays and lesbians and they might be clueless about what bisexual means, they might think that I am making this up and I am a confused guy.

Initially, when I felt attracted to guys I felt like I was gay because I have feelings towards boys and it took me a while to accept my feelings that it is perfectly alright to have feelings towards other men and it is okay to be gay.

Sometime later I realized that I feel the same way about girls the way I feel about boys and at this point, I was totally confused and I thought I was having some kind of mental crisis. I used to think that I could not be attracted to both genders as it is not possible to feel attracted to both genders.

So I had to choose between feeling attracted to boys and girls and it was a tough decision because I liked both genders I was having a tough time deciding on this and then years later I realized that I was wrong all the time.

I don't have to choose between the 2 and I can be with any gender I want provided the fact that they accept me. I had accepted myself and I was glad that my confusion was cleared later, I think several people feel confused about their sexuality.

Although every human is different and every case is even different if you ever feel confused about your sexuality, see that if you can talk to someone because if you are within yourself then you might have so many doubts and it will hamper your overall confidence and you will start to doubt yourself.

I know sometimes the help is far away and we might think that we are lonely and we are not supposed to talk about this but trust me you should try talking to someone. You must make some quality friends and spend some time otherwise it can eat you from the inside.

You might feel alienated and the world does not love you and care about you but I don't think that world is such a horrible place, yes it is a horrible place but it is also a place where you can meet some good people no matter what you are going through.

If you can't afford to go to therapy you can always find friends and hang out with them and if you feel comfortable you could tell the story you always were hiding or had to hide because you felt some people would judge you.

This is not a foolproof way but I think it is a great way of spending time instead of being within yourself and overthinking, you could spend some time with others and it will probably make you feel less bad about yourselves.

Although I am not a mental health expert I think that socializing can make you feel good about yourself and people who feel alienated tend to feel lonely and their brain starts to act in weird ways. If you look at it from your psychological perspective, our brain is heavily dependent on the hormones it releases.

It is up to me what kind of activity I do because the type of activity I do different hormones are going to release and it will have different impacts. So for a change, I will have to go out and do something positive and hope that I will receive positive from the other end.

Although the hope is a great thing things don't always go as expected I think this is the way one should follow if we want to get some good results sometimes things are not that easy but we have to strive for the good and hope that something good happens to us.

Anyways coming back to bisexuals, I think it is important that we should know the myths and struggles related to it and how their problems are quite different from their counterparts. They face different kinds of problems when compared with gays and lesbians.

I think the biggest problem they face is the dilemma of whether or not they should reveal the secret because in case they do not reveal the secret it is not as if their truth is going to get exposed unless they do something really stupid no one is going to know the fact that they are bisexual and I am starting to realize that I do have an advantage.

I can be bisexual and not let anyone know that I am bisexual and can lead a double life of pretending to be a heterosexual person and leading a normal life like others and no one would know a thing, a feature which is not available to other folks who are not bisexual.

Although I do not want to lead a life in case I have to get married to someone I would be glad if I could make a full discourse to someone who wants to spend the rest of her life with me because it would feel like I am betraying them if I am not telling them what my sexuality is and if she still accepts I would be more than happy to be her mate for life.

At the end of the day, truth is very important to me because often we feel that no one can know the reality but eventually it comes out through an unknown source which might make me feel uncomfortable and I do not want my partner to discover the truth from any other source other than me because if she does, she might never be able to trust me again.

I think our lives might be different but there might be a few common things among us. It is important that how despite our lives being different could have been a lot worse but I think we should be thankful that we are alive and happy in bits and pieces.

Although I think that bisexuals might have some advantages when they are compared to gays and lesbians, their lives is not so easy. I am not saying this because I am bisexual and I want everyone to be sympathetic towards but I think this is the reality.

Yes, probably a lot of guys and girls might be secretly bisexual or even bi-curious without their partner finding out. They could be in a serious heterosexual relationship and might be keeping things to themselves so that things don't get messier and to a large extent they might even get away with it.

In the past few years more than gays and lesbians, I was able to connect to a lot of bisexual people online and I was really surprised to see the number of people I found online but I think it is not that hard for them and they could swing both ways and no one would notice.

Since they are attracted to both genders they are less likely to get caught by their family members or friends and even if they are caught in some compromising situation they can make something up so that no one would suspect them because everyone thinks that they are straight.

It all looks great for a bisexual person, I mean they need not stress about their secret getting exposed and they can pretend to be straight person, be in a relationship like normal guys maybe engage in some homosexual encounters and life might be so smooth for them but often it is not that smooth for them.

I think there is a reason why a lot of bisexual people get alienated and feel lonely. First of all, very few people have heard of the term as many people are ignorant of the term. They have heard of the term gay and that's it and for them anyone who behaves weirdly in a sexual way considers that person to be gay.

Unfortunately, so many people don't even know what a lesbian means or even heard of that term and they have no idea about bisexuality and are quite ignorant on this subject. Even if you tell someone that you are bisexual they probably would not even understand because they have never heard of it and they have never thought of it.

You will have a tough time explaining to them how bisexuality means getting attracted to both genders and it is perfectly normal to have the same kind of feelings towards both genders. I think at this point most would be awestruck that such a phenomenon can also exist because they have been ignorant all their life and they would think that it is not possible.

This is not a far-stretched idea several of the people you meet would give you the same response and would say stuff like "ok so you are both straight and gay, why do you like both genders, it is not possible to like both genders."

These are some of the common responses you would hear or most likely hear if they confess that they are bisexual. The biggest problem is that not only do they consider being gay something unnatural and disease, but they also refuse to acknowledge bisexuality as it is something worse than being gay.

The most unfortunate thing is the response that is given to bisexual people from their community ie., by gays and lesbians predominantly because they feel that bisexuals have it easy in the world and since they are part straight so we are not part of this community.

So we are alienated by our own and we are alienated by the outsiders, I think one thing I do not like about this community is the way they treat us. Yes, there might be a few advantages but there are lots of ways we are disadvantaged.

I think a lot of people who have closely followed LGBT stuff have written tons of articles on it on how bisexuals get alienated by its people how they are considered a part of their community and how their mental health is being affected by it.

I think at the end of the day we have to realize, despite our sexuality being different there are some things in which we are similar. Although my struggles do not match your struggles at the end of the day it is tough being bisexual and even if you come out as bisexual, there are so many questions people have for you, some are silly some are valid.

Although I think there is an injustice that is happening to the LGBT community around the world and how certain stereotypes are causing a lot of damage I think it is also important to note the fact of the mistreatment of our own. Many people might disagree with a few things I just said but I think this is indeed a reality and when I read some articles online it might be true.

Online articles are not enough to assert a certain fact but personal life experience along with the people I have met online and the experiences they have shared with me makes me think that there might be some truth behind it. Maybe they are right and maybe it is high time we have been saying about stuff which has been externally hurting but maybe we should look internally as well.

Now I am not pointing fingers at anything but sometimes things are not as easy as they seem sometimes we are focused so much on fighting outside that we forget certain things which go out of order and can cause chaos. I think it is worth looking into it as things are usually complicated and it will not harm us.

We have been fighting for such a long period and we have been calling spade a spade no matter which religion gender or ideology they might support, this is what I like the most about our community. They would never compromise our community in the name of fighting for the greater good, I think our morality is much more than that of an average person.

This might be offensive to a lot of people who are not from the LGBT community and I don't mean to hurt them but my only intention is to point out that our intentions have been straight from the start and we don't desire money or politics.

We are here for awareness and if we can do that we don't care who we have to offend. Whether you are left, right or centre-leaning they are of the same people to me and as long as you respect me the same thing will be provided to you but if you can't then you won't receive it from my end and I am not partial towards any ideology.

If you hate homosexuals, I don't care what ideology you believe in and how you are making it a safe place for you and your friends all I care about is that you are not my well-wisher and I would never respect you and I would never trust you and honestly I would not even care about because you never really cared about me or what I represent.

I am saying this because often people expect to give a free pass to certain individuals because they belong to a certain ideology and since they are fighting their struggles, I should just shut up and make sure that I don't speak against that person as that person is fighting much bigger battles than me.

I am sorry to say but I cannot respect such individuals who engage in this kind of behaviour where they say something against homosexuals. They still call themselves some kind of messiah of the oppressed and you are certainly not my messiah.

There might be folks who might be interested in you and maybe a lot of activists might be around you and make you feel good but I don't think I can be around such people because they are fake and hypocrites according to me and they will do whatever gives them money and I certainly cannot respect such a person who is blind towards money that they betray their ideology.

Hopefully, others can understand what I am trying to say, I do not want to point at people as it is not a wise thing to do but at the end of the day I have to say some things which might be a little bit harsh and uncomfortable and probably some might even get angry at me for saying such things because it is kind of forbidden but then again I don't care much.

Again I feel there have been issues of infighting which should be avoided but there are cases where it is quite visible about certain stereotypes that are being mainstreamed and the kind of criticism we get from our own is kind of shocking.

Despite all our differences, I think it is important that we focus on real issues. If we keep blaming each other and doing the same thing that the others are trying to do then we are losing the plot, it is crucial that we focus on who the actual enemy is and it is not a fellow person whose sexuality might be a little different.

At the end of the day even if our sexualities are different there might be a growing feeling that if you are not gay you might not understand the pain of a gay man and if you are not a lesbian you might not understand the pain of them and similarly, bisexuals might be having a similar feeling and not to mention transgender who always feel left behind.

There is some growing discontent when it comes to our community, yes there are so many nice things about us but there are some concerns which need to be addressed and since we are fighting a lot of things no one cares to address these matters as they are not our top priority.

I think it is crucial that no one feels that they are left behind or they feel that they are being exploited. We all have a different role to play, we might have some hard feelings for each other and that is alright. We cannot like and love everyone and we must keep whatever grudges we hold against each other aside and think calmly for a while.

Every action has some consequence and if we keep fighting among ourselves we can never focus on our real target, our target is not to fight amongst each other as it may cause more damage than we had intended.

Our real target has and should always be those ignorant people who don't like us or hate us we have to take them and show that we are not some kind of weak people they can play whenever they want we are here and we will not go a step back and we must be able to add more and more members to the community because that is how we are going to win this narrative.

They want us to feel that we are not important and we somehow don't matter and our lives don't matter but I think they matter for a lot of people and slowly things are changing, in the past, we were able to change the mindset of a few folks, there have been a lot of people who are supportive of us and in future, a lot more of them are going to support us and that is what matters the most.

We can put aside all the other things, this is our moment and never we might have had this chance before. I know what so many people are thinking that no one cares about us and it is just us and some of the supporters but I think this time it is just more than that.

I think often we feel that we are marginalized and from time to time that is indeed true but I think at times we can focus on big things and make sure that we focus on our goals. Although each person has a different goal from their sexual point of view as a community our goal should be to make it a safer place for everyone.

A lot of us belong to different professions, we come from different backgrounds and might even have different ideologies but despite all this, if we can focus it on a particular thing or a goal then it would be great.

Everyone has their own set of problems but despite all these problems if we are truly committed to it then we can make a lot of difference because there are people out there who need our help and it should be our top priority that we should help them because there are hundreds of such kids who need our help.

At times they might not be able to reach us but we have to make a platform in such a way that we create an environment where they feel comfortable and they can reach out to us or they can come out in the open with their sexuality without any fear of getting threatened or killed by the people around them.

Although it seems like that day is very far before such a thing happens I think it is important that we take baby steps there are already so many people who are doing this activism and I feel great and honoured that such people exist and they are helping for our cause.

Although their work has never reached me I am sure it might have reached a lot of people who are in need and maybe we need to support in whatever we can to these organizations. There are a lot of activists some are gay and lesbian activists while others are transgender activists.

Everyone is trying their best to achieve their desired goals because we have people who are confused and they have no one to consult. If they can act as mentors and maybe guide them in the right direction then we would be doing a favour to a lot of people.

I know a lot of people who think that if their child turns out like that they should somehow disown them or the kid is of no use and dead to them which can cause a lot of trauma. I think there are tons of which are wrong and need to be addressed and one thing which needs to be addressed is some of the aggressive thinking.

I have seen a lot of folks who are very aggressive when it comes to dealing with homosexuals and sometimes they even get emotional to the point they start doing things which might not make sense to a lot of people.

As I have discussed earlier there is a fear among your family members and that is one of the major reasons why they act in such a weird way because they have a tough time believing that their son or daughter could have such sexuality.

One thing I have learned about suppressing things is that the more you try to suppress it better its chances of coming out. So, the folks who think that intimidating or hurting someone will stop them are wrong. The more you try to stop your kids from doing it, the more will be curiosity and curiosity is a dangerous thing and can cause a lot of damage.

You are thinking that if I tell my children not to do it or if I can stop it by hook or by crook you have succeeded in having what you want and you may succeed at some level but eventually, things are not going to go the same way. I think there is going to be a tsunami of people who are going homosexual or bisexual.

You can stop maybe 10 or 12 people but when they are hundreds and thousands in numbers then you can only wonder what went wrong. You would be starting to wonder if your parenting has failed or if is this due to westernization of the society. Either way, things are not going your way and the number of our community goes strong, the more it will be difficult for the other side to stop us.

I think all these years we have lived in fear and struggled with a lot of things but I think that our moment has truly come and if we have to ever make a difference and show everyone that we are an essential part of this society and no matter how hard you try you cannot change your sexuality with your morality.

Slowly things are changing although we have not yet fully gained our rights and still it is a long way to go I think we are going in the right direction. When we did not have the numbers it was a really tough time but slowly times are changing although we might be outnumbered by many the positive thing is that we have allies and we have support of people from our community.

I think the next 10 years or so belongs to us, so we must make full use of it. There is still a lot of work that needs to be done. Some people are doing things and making it happen in their field and trying to make it a better environment for everyone and hopefully whoever is involved in this campaign achieves the success they are looking for.

IX

Acceptance

Acceptance is a very strong thing, I mean if we look at it in our day-to-day life we have so many things we have to seek acceptance. Life is a mystery after all, we learn so many things and every day is a new day where we might learn something new.

Even if we look from a layman's perspective, accepting something new can be hard after all I think a lot of us are conservative when it comes to a lot of things and we have a tough time accepting what we feel is unnatural or something completely new or unheard.

I think before we talk about accepting LGBT people in our life, I think it is important that we talk about how difficult acceptance can be from the human perspective and usually what are the things that our brain faces from denial to the acceptance stage.

Sometimes when we look at everything from one perspective we might not understand things but if we start to look at certain things from multiple perspectives then we can see the reality and maybe understand why certain things should be seen in that way and maybe we can understand how hard it is because it is much more hard than it seems.

From time to time, we are faced with new challenges in our lives everyone has their own set of philosophies and each person has a different approach to life so he/she will face the challenge in their way and try to solve it in their way.

I think till here everyone would agree that any person with whatever ideology would do the same thing. To be frank I don't like change and I can understand why some people have a problem with change. You start to think that once you have changed a little eventually everything about you will be changed and maybe you start to doubt yourself.

This is in my opinion why people don't want acceptance and I am not accepting someone who is of LGBT background but sometimes the truth is so hurtful that you don't want to accept it as you don't want to feel bad as it hurts you and you do not want to go through that hurt.

Let's just say that you love a person very closely and then that person ends up dead and accepting that person is gone can take some time. You can accept within one hour, one day, one week, one month or sometimes more than one month depending on the person and the kind of feelings they have.

It is not easy accepting the death of a loved one, often people go in shock, and they might have to go to therapy so that they can come out of it. I have seen people for days they cannot do their normal day-to-day activities which they were able to do quite easily because something so terrible has happened that every moment is really hard for them.

Now the reason I am giving the example of acceptance of your dead one is because I have experienced it in my personal life and I had a tough time accepting it for a long period I could not accept it and even if I was able to accept it I just didn't know what I should do with this because it was shocking.

I am sure other people who have lost their loved ones and had a tough time accepting their loss because it is so hard to accept the reality because one moment you are talking to them and another moment everything is gone and now all you have is their memories.

Most people usually accept the loss within a given period, some people might take more time than others as they do not want to accept the reality as the truth is not something you want to accept and it is something which makes you feel bad but no matter how hard you try you cannot change the reality.

In the beginning, it will hurt and then you will begin to live with that hurt and slowly you are going to accept that the person is gone and depending upon your beliefs you might have different ideas about where that person might have gone. One certain thing is that once a person is dead they are not going to come back and whether you like it or not you will start to realize it.

There might be times when certain things might remind you of that person but eventually, you will learn to accept it is a slow and gradual process it is surprising that there were sleepless nights for me and I used to overthink a lot and then it took a while for me to understand that no matter how hard I try the reality is not going to change.

I might think that I can change the truth but I cannot change it as I am powerless over these things and no human is that strong they bring back their loved ones certainly I don't possess those powers so I gave up and yes there was a bit of sadness, shock and grief.

I started to realize that I was going from bad to worse, I was having all kinds of thoughts. There were moments when I was starting to feel restless and empty and even though I tried to keep busy myself there were several moments which made me realize that I was lonely and it was starting to hit me badly.

People say that you have to move on from an incident and no matter how hard something stings you just can't keep it and let it hit you because you have to keep moving forward and forget it as a bad memory I was hoping that since time is such a great healer, all that pain that was there it would slowly vanish or I would be able to accept my pain because I am not great at accepting things.

Although our topic is quite different from what I am talking but I think that there is an important lesson for everyone here. If you are someone who readily accepts the truth or if you are someone who does not easily accept the truth the lesson to be learned is that there are some harsh realities of life which take time to understand.

We might not get it at one time sometimes it takes time to understand a certain thing and that is the reason I had to give the example of death because a lot of people have seen their loved ones die at some point and no matter what your ideology is you might be close to that one or maybe two people in your life.

When they die there is some sort of emptiness within them for a while and eventually, you accept the truth or find ways to accept the truth. I think the point I am trying to make is that acceptance can be really hard and for someone ignorant and hateful I think it would take a lot of processing to accept the reality.

Now in the case of the person who is dead even if you want to avoid reality it is crystal clear that the person is dead and although you want to change it, it is out of your hands so no matter what you do you cannot change it and that is why the person has no chance but to accept that the person they love so dearly is dead and is not going to come back.

Now compare this to a situation where an individual wants to come out as gay or lesbian or any other sexuality, then the situation is completely different and the scenarios are completely different. The other person can change you by force; they need not accept you for what you are and might use forceful ways to make sure that you drop the idea.

This is not the first time that such a scenario has been played and I can only imagine what it could be often it is not that hard to imagine because you usually get the same type of answer, and if you surround yourself with people who hate homosexuals in general then there is not much you can do.

In most families, these people are outnumbered. Hence, the chance of getting your point is next to impossible and you should consider yourself lucky if you are not physically beaten because there are lots of myths regarding homosexuality seen among a lot of people.

There are families I have seen with my own eyes who think that if something bad is happening to your childhood then he/she is a victim of some kind of ghost and you need to go to some tantrik to get that ghost out of it. I have seen several people do this kind of stuff and it is crazy the number of people who believe in this kind of shit.

Although their parents had not suspected them of being homosexual often they would engage in stuff that they would find odd and feel that their kids were slipping out of their hands they took their kids to the Tantrik and they would do some crazy shit to take the ghost and spirit out of them.

If you are one of those people who don't know what a Tantrik is then let me shortly explain you. A Tantrik is usually someone who does magic and they are considered dangerous and mysterious people generally, there is a strong belief that if you are not able to cure something then you have to go to this Tantrik guy to cure that person.

You could say that it is equivalent to someone doing Voodoo shit, I don't know how many people believe in Voodoo but I guess you can understand what I am trying to say. Anyways those Tantrik guys do some crazy shit they would often torture people just to get the ghost out of a certain person.

Most of the time they physically beat a person or they make someone touch a hot object which might cause danger to the bodies. Some of the cases have been so severe that small kids have died due to this tantrik because they were trying to ghost out of some kid who was not displaying normal behaviour.

I know that this might be shocking to a lot of people but I have gone to these places so it was not shocking to me as I grew some visuals were so haunting in nature that doing some out-of-the-ordinary was out of the question and we would never think of doing something like that because the consequences were going to be very severe.

Now obviously I am telling you just a few experiences I had and based on those experiences I was sure that if someone knows that their kid is homosexual. Most of the people in India come from small towns and villages their first reaction is to take their kid to their hometown and get them cured because even if you are living in urban areas you don't expect a solution in the city.

And I am pretty sure that not all parents are like these but some of the people from the middle class and lower middle class are like these and I am not narrating these stories to scare them but to tell them that is one reality which I have seen and they could face too if they come from a similar background.

If your parents are not like this then I guess you are very lucky and if the majority of parents don't behave like this then I guess I have the wrong picture of most people and if they accept you for what you are then you are living among really great people and I just hope there are more people like your family.

And if you happen to belong to a family that doesn't accept you then there are only a few options that are available to you. One option is that you could just run away from the house and start a new life and hope that they would never find you but it is easier said than done.

Even if you try to run away from your family, there is a high probability they can find you and what happens next is completely unpredictable, even if they forget about you and think that you are dead, it is not easy starting from scratch and you have to make sure that you have a place to live and you have to find a place to work and not to mention you have to make new friends.

As easy as it may sound, doing it, in reality, is tough and for a bachelor, it is pretty bad to get a place to live because no one trusts bachelors these days and it can get tough for you to get a place to live if you get married by chance then the situation becomes easier because that's how society works I guess.

If you are a homosexual then you cannot get married so there is no escape for you and even if you manage to rent a place there is a high probability that your neighbours could find out about your sexuality as the neighbours can be nosy at times and if you are getting old they might want you to get married as soon as possible.

This shit used to happen to me at my workplace as I was constantly reminded that I have to get married sooner or later this topic was brought up by my coworkers and just like my family I used to change goal posts thinking that one day they would stop talking about it but they never learned.

If you live in an apartment or some gated community then the chances are that once the news gets leaked it will eventually travel to everyone and maybe you will have to pack your bags and go somewhere else because there are very few places you would find people where societies accept homosexuals and they don't want trouble so they simply do not want you living there.

It could be disheartening to see that these kinds of incidents are happening or can happen daily and now I come to my original point, that if you are thinking of running away from your family and then starting from zero it would be much more complicated than you would think.

Not to mention that going to a new place and finding a job is in itself a callous thing to do and if you are planning to go to a metro city then your difficulties will increase. The cost of living in big cities is much more than your small city and managing your expenses can get tricky when you have no one who can support you financially and emotionally.

At the end of the day, it is not impossible but I don't think everyone is capable of doing it, some can pull it off but you have to be prepared for the worst. The second option is that you will have to convince your family that they have to accept your sexuality and it does not matter whether they like it because they cannot control your life.

It is your life and once you turn 18 only you should be able to decide what you have to do with your life whether it is your career or your sexuality. In all probability, your family would not want to accept you because as I said earlier they think that you seem to have some kind of mental illness and they have this moral responsibility to treat you.

It is a tough situation for any person and if you happen to be among those people who are still a teenager and have a tough time managing your expenses it is going to get tough for you and usually, there is not much you can do.

If you are an independent person then that is a separate story but if you are not then there is not much you can do, in this kind of situation the best thing you can do is just not tell anyone because if you do you would jeopardise your entire life so it is always better to be safe than sorry.

I know that there is a lot of burden particularly among teenagers and they want to get this thing out of their chest and do it once it for all and bear the consequences but I think it all depends on your surroundings if your environment you can tell them but if you are living in a hostile environment then I would suggest you to think twice before doing something.

You should not be doing something in a hurry as we don't know what will happen and ultimately at the end of the day you are the boss and you have every right to do what you want but I think as a well-wisher I can only say something which I feel is the best for a certain individual in a certain situation.

I can be wrong and I don't want anyone to blindly follow anything because if we blindly follow anyone's advice usually we get stuck at a point and once we are stuck at that point we have no one to guide us and then you will have to use your brain and it will generate a new outcome which you would not be expecting.

Anything I say through this book is only for reading and if you feel that some of the things that I mentioned can be used in real life try to use it without caution because often I would say something but the execution happens in a different way than it should be and then if you come to me for further advice so I won't be able to help you out.

So if you are taking something which I have written as advice please be careful and use it at your own risk because I cannot be held liable afterwards because I cannot be responsible for something which I have said in ideal conditions and your conditions might differ from that.

You have to be very careful while reading online advice because I am not a therapist or professional and I don't think my advice should be considered as a substitute for some kind of therapy because everything you do has some other consequence and I don't want to set a bad example.

If someone tries to take an example and tries to do something and it backfires let's just say that the media reports that they got inspired because someone had read something in a book then I would feel bad and maybe guilty because I have set something in motion which I could not control and I lost control of it.

Now if such information does get out then it could damage me emotionally so whatever you do think properly before taking any advice just like that. Analyse it and see if that thing suits your situation and try to imagine the reactions if you do a particular action i think it will surely help you in these kinds of situations.

This should apply to all kinds of things you read online or someone telling you something because you are the one to bear the consequences and usually that person who has given advice just raises their hand and does not want to be held accountable and it is quite understandable that you do not want to be in such a situation.

That being said I think acceptance of your sexuality does have a lot to do with psychology and if we go by psychological perspective then the people who don't accept your sexuality are the ones either afraid of you or jealous of you.

Before someone goes into complete panic mode let me explain to you a little background before I will explain it. We need to talk about both these emotions fear and jealousy. Both the emotions of fear and jealousy have a connection and they are interconnected.

Fear is one of the most complicated emotions because you have all the roller coaster things going on in your mind and fear is both a good and bad thing. If we look at it from a psychological perspective then fear stems out of hatred and you just hate that thing so much that you seem to have negative feelings in your mind.

Once you start to have negative feelings towards a person or object then it lives in your head rent-free which can cause all kinds of chemical reactions in your body and can result in giving you an emotion called fear. I know that a lot of people associate fear with being weak and not able to withstand something but if you look closer then the reality is something else.

Fear has a very close relationship with hate and when hate cannot make you win you start to fear that person I am sure everyone might have hated someone so much that they start to fear, if you start to think then I am sure some person would pop in your mind instantly.

Probably when you were a kid or a teenager there was someone who you didn't like and eventually, you were starting to feel afraid of that person in your heart. You might not like being scared of that person like you wanted to run away but there was a feeling in your heart of being uneasy in seeing that person because you don't like that person.

Eventually, the hatred turns into fear and you start to avoid the person because you are afraid of the kind of interactions you would have with this person slowly you come to a situation where if that person you strongly dislike is around you there might be a change in some hormones in your body and your heart starts to race.

Now coming to jealousy, I think this emotion is much easier to understand but it is a complex emotion because sometimes the kind of people who are jealous of you makes you wonder if jealousy emotion has some kind of logic attached to it or if is it completely illogical.

If we go by definition then jealousy is a feeling if you are feeling bad because someone is really happy or their circumstances are much better than yours. You feel bad about yourself and you try to compare your life with others and come to the conclusion that your life is not good and hence you are now jealous of a person, group or community.

Now going by this definition it should mean that anyone jealous, their life is supposedly in a bad phase and whoever they are feeling jealous about is in a good phase. The person then sees how bad or pathetic their life is and then tries to do a series of things that can make them feel good.

To feel good they can spread some rumours, talk behind their back or try to do little harm by endangering the surroundings around them or maybe create misunderstanding between their friends and family or try to do some illegal things so that the jealous person can go ahead and win this thing.

Usually, we assume that the jealous person is poorer than they are jealous of or they are not as beautiful compared to the person of whom they are feeling jealous but turns out this is not true you can actually feel jealous of a person who is probably much less wealthy than you and probably has better life but they just can't stand the sight of you being happy.

I think I have done a fair job of explaining both the emotions called fear and jealousy and how they are related to each other. I think almost everyone who hates homosexuals comes into the category although there might be some people who don't fit in that category but currently, we have to focus on the majority of folks.

If you look at the majority of the people who hate homosexuals or disapprove of them follow a similar pattern, they all display similar characteristics. All of them have displayed that there is a bit of fear and jealousy when it comes to homosexuals.

Now anyone would ask why they would be afraid or jealous of homosexuals when in reality they hate homosexuals. The statement may not make sense to a lot of people but they are afraid that by seeing you someone else from the family might take inspiration and follow on the same path.

They just hate the fact you have so much power to influence someone without actually trying to intentionally do it. They are afraid of a scenario where more people might start to become homosexuals and once it happens they do not want this to happen.

This is not an ideal scenario for them because since childhood they have been taught only one thing how homosexuals are bad people and anyone who is behaving very weirdly might be a homosexual there are several myths related to homosexuals that people believe to be true.

A lot of people are afraid of homosexuals for some reason, this fear is very prominent among a lot of people. As a kid, I was told to avoid homosexuals for some reason initially I did not understand why they were so scared of homosexuals. When I was a teenager I was told that they are capable of doing wrong things to you sexually and would try to exploit you.

I am pretty sure that there have been a lot of families who have been told that they should avoid homosexuals at all costs as they are really bad people. Usually, this kind of stereotyping arises from ignorance, I think we need to teach them what homosexuality is and what it is not.

The only way to tackle homophobia is to re-educate and if there are people who want to kill you just because you are homosexual I think they don't deserve to be in a civil society because they are very dangerous people. I don't know why but so many people are against homosexuality sometimes I have a tough time understanding this hate.

People make different choices in their entire lifetime but no one questions them the moment it comes to sexuality suddenly everyone becomes a mom and starts to monitor stuff that I am doing which is bad and should not happen at any cost.

Everyone should have a moment of privacy and what I do in my private life is my thing and no one should be able to question me or my morality because if we start to question everyone's life choices then we would end up nowhere. It would be just a bunch of nosy people trying to pull each other down.

I think it is best for everyone if we stay out of personal lives out of each other. As long we are not harming each other then it is okay that we do not like each other. Even if you hate a certain community that is also fine up to a certain extent but if you start to go violent against us then things are going to get complicated.

I think one of the biggest reasons why people think that they could do these horrible things and get away with it is because they have no fear of consequences and in a country like India where people take everything for granted including things such as law, privacy etc.

But I think times are changing more and more number people are actively coming out and supporting this movement and maybe in the future we will see a lesser number of bullying cases as we are forced to see.

I see a brighter future for this movement and all those people who hate homosexuals or any other sexuality I have nothing to say at this moment because I am a patient man I would be waiting to see till the tables are turned and when once the tables are turned in our favour it would be a rather interesting conversation to have.

I know that so many people get pissed off just to see so many homosexuals out there and when things will start to get normalised then it would be an even worse time for them. I think homophobes are afraid of homosexuals not in a frightening way but enough to cause heartburn in them and there will come a day when they will feel powerless.

I hope that day comes soon because they had enjoyed this power for centuries and toyed with a lot of people for decades and centuries and now they are pissed off that the narrative they had is slowly fading away. The newer generation does not hate homosexuals the same way they used to hate and they don't like it.\

They also hate the fact that even if the newer generation are straight they are supporting this movement, they can understand homosexuals supporting each other but the fact that someone who is not a homosexual is also supporting this movement can be a little tricky for them.

They are unable to digest the fact that people are accepting homosexuality and homosexuals and there are a lot of people who are openly supporting gay, lesbian, bisexual, transgender, queer and other sexualities. People are confident and they are not shying away from this.

I think in the coming to few generations the hatred against homosexuals or LGBT, in general, will go down and all the activists who are fighting for us can hope to create a society where the kids are not afraid to come out and no one hunts them down just for being a little different than others.

X
What's Next

If you have read the previous 9 chapters then I think I should congratulate you because you might have read a lot of things which might made sense to you but probably some of the things didn't make sense to you and you could not understand what I was trying to say.

I think there might be a few things you were able to understand and a few things you could not understand and I think that is perfectly alright because I understand that a lot of times my point of view can be a little hard to understand and it has nothing to do with you or your knowledge but has everything to do with me.

You see if you look at my personal life then I can be a hard fellow to understand. A lot of people want to understand me and they are usually disappointed in me because they have a tough time following logic and the reasoning behind the things I do.

I accept that I can be a pain in the ass and a lot of people dislike me because often I display behaviour which is not considered normal. I have been getting these kinds of comments all my life and initially, I used to feel bad but now I don't feel bad at all.

I do not know if any other people who are from the LGBT community receive similar kinds of comments but I have been receiving such comments for a long time and I can only imagine the kind of comments I would be receiving if they got to know that I am bisexual.

It is kind of crazy that I don't want to imagine such a scenario because I know the kind of impact I have on people and it is not a pleasant experience with me so I can understand if while reading the book some of the things I said made you uncomfortable or you could not even relate with certain things with what I was saying.

It is certainly possible that you may not understand what I was saying through different chapters of the book and I may also not understand certain topics because our experiences might be different how we view certain things can be different and that is the reason why certain people can have different opinions.

You can agree with certain points with what I am saying, you can agree with everything that I am saying, you can disagree with certain points I am saying and you can disagree with everything I am saying. All these scenarios are possible for any individual that is reading my book and I don't have a problem with any of these possibilities.

I am open to all kinds of possibilities which is what makes this special. Even if you hated some of the points which I said you still read it till the end then I am grateful to the reader that they had the patience before abruptly stopping reading and making a harsh judgement on me and my book.

Now that you have made it this far I want to discuss a special topic which is quite different from what I have discussed so far. So far we have discussed gays, lesbians, bisexuals and transgenders here and there.

I know that a lot of people want me to discuss transgenders because a lot of times they feel neglected by society and often they have a lot of complaints against the society. I agree that transgenders are an important part of the community but the reason I have not discussed is that I believe that it is a sensitive area and I probably should not talk about it.

There are certain things for which I might get a lot of earful and people might start to hate me for doing those things and I don't want to ruin a book experience for a lot of people. At the end of the day, certain things are said in mainstream media which I disagree with and I will continue to hold those arguments for a lot of time.

I know that I should be honest about these things and I should probably give my opinion but I think it is best for everyone if we only discuss homosexuals and bisexuals as they are much simpler topics to discuss in comparison to transgender.

Probably a lot of people wanted me to discuss transgender and the role they play in this community and how they form an important part of this community but there is not much you can do about it because this is my book and you will have to respect my wishes. You might not like that aspect but I believe that the decision I took is the right one.

I know that a lot of people might even start to make a lot of assumptions about me that I don't like transgender or I might hate them or I might be having some kind of issue with them but that is not the case. I have read about transgender and its rights very carefully and I think we are treading on thin ice when it comes to transgenders.

Probably that is the reason that I did not talk about it as I did not think it was right on my part to discuss it as a layman because at the end of the day, I am a layman talking about different sexualities and now you would think that if that is the case why I have written so much about homosexuals and bisexuals.

Well, the answer is quite simple it is because I identify as bisexual and I used to consider myself a homosexual at one point in time I think that I can tell things and share my experience and I feel that I have earned my right to talk about it.

I know that this answer is not satisfactory to a lot of people, some people might feel that I have not been fully honest some might feel that I am lying and I may not be able to change the way you think and feel about me even I were to write an entire book on clarify my opinion on transgender.

I think I have said enough on this topic and no matter what you think what I said is gonna matter much. I said what I felt was right hopefully we can move on from here. I know that this chapter is pretty much boring and it feels like a mixture of recap, and me trying to justify myself anyway I had some different ideas about what I wanted to talk about.

I wanted to focus more on what we can do from here, in all these chapters we discussed definitions experiences and different aspects that homosexuals and bisexuals have to go through but I think it is important that we discuss what we can do from here.

Even if you are someone who used to homosexuals and now no longer hates them you would be asking what is the next step for us. I think the next step for us is to educate as many people as we can in whatever way we can.

I am of the firm belief that we can change people's mindset through education and what you are educating about really matters. The content matters and if the content is really good then it can cause a lot of disruptions but if your content is not that good even if you are talking about a noble cause it can make it look like a bad thing.

I think visual media is the king as of now, look at YouTube and Instagram. There are influencers or whatever you call the people who make content on YouTube are making a lot of difference. The harsh reality is that no one reads anymore and everyone likes to watch and read and probably that is the reason Amazon Audible is so famous.

There are so many YouTube channels that have become famous, some of these YouTubers have much more impact than mainstream media and the same goes for the creators on Instagram. For some reason, social media seems to have trumped the mainstream and a lot of people love it more than mainstream media.

There seems to be mistrust between people and mainstream media and that is the reason we see so many people who seem to not like people from mainstream media. It does not matter what ideology you follow but you have to agree to the fact that there has been a lot of propaganda in your mainstream media.

There have been several occasions where your mainstream media people have lied straight to your faces and that has to be the number 1 reason behind this mistrust as a lot of folks think that they will do whatever the corporation tells them to do. The corporation does whatever fetches them more money and they don't seem to care much about anything.

So now you have small creators, people who are not funded by corporations but rather have a small team and mostly survive on YouTube money or the donations they seek online. They might not be 100% honest people but their reputation is certainly better than those new anchors who seem to cannot have their opinion on a certain matter.

I don't have anything against books or reading, I love books and reading but we have to face some realities as well. The biggest reality in our face today is that most people don't read and they might not even have the patience to read. Maybe some people do have the time but nowadays people are busy.

Most people are so busy that they might not have time to read an entire chapter and forget about reading an entire book and even if they read the number of people who do that is very low. I have seen people around me spend hours and hours watching videos but they won't even read for 10 mins.

If you look at it from a psychological point of view then I think one of the biggest reasons why prefer like to watch than read is because while reading you have to make an active effort but while watching you don't have to make any effort. You just have to play a video and the rest will be done by your ears and brain.

When I had a job, we would often talk about marketing in several of our meetings and one thing which was constantly agreed upon was the kind of impact the visual medium has upon the people and why so many of the marketing people focus so much on creating videos rather than writing something.

According to them, you are more likely to watch a short video compared to reading 4 to 5 lines, if you have 4 to 5 lines and you convert it into a short video then your engagement ratio is likely to be much higher. The reason I decided to write this book is to not become the #1 author or something because I am aware that I will not become a top author.

The reason for me writing this book is that I want to focus on all the things through which we can bring awareness among the people who don't like homosexuals and writing a book was among them. I felt that there are not many books written at least in India on this topic so this book might appeal to a lot of book readers.

Even if this book turns out to be a flop I would not mind it because this is just one of the things that I had in mind after this I will look for opportunities in the visual medium and see the things I would be able to create and whether or not I am creative enough to be a content creator and survive in that world only time will tell.

I am telling you about this because I hardly see any people from the LGBT community on the internet and even if they are present they seem to write instead of creating content. Different channels talk about politics, religion and other topics. There are YouTube channels which talk about different movies and TV shows and dissect their ideology.

There are lots of channels which talk about their opinions and it sounds great but I can barely see anyone talking about the issues of LGBT people and even if there are channels which discuss the plight of these people, they are barely visible and very few channels exist.

I don't know how many people tried to make content of this type but I think we can reach a lot of people if we make educational videos or videos related to homosexuality and other stuff and can discuss the current scenario and legal help of those kids who are having a lot of problems in their personal life.

I know that initially it is a bit tough and you will face a lot of anger and hate comments from a lot of people but that happens with a lot of creators initially you would struggle and might face a backlash but eventually you will find people who agree with you and who would appreciate you.

I think it is a great time for us to be alive as the creators who want to focus on these themes have so much to do and they have a wide range of audience. If for some reason this book does not reach that many people or it does not even get published.

Yes, there is a chance that this book might not even get published because I have never written anything in my life and this is my first stint as a writer. I don't even know the kind of mistakes I might have made as a writer and since this is the first time there are a lot of things I am unsure about.

I think that is okay that I am unsure about so many things because I am not a pro writer maybe I am not a good writer or maybe I need some pointers to be a good writer. I don't even know about the future of what I have written I will try to get it published and I don't know if anyone is going to publish my book.

I don't have contacts within the writing and publishing industry and I am pretty sure that no one knows me so I guess I will let the fate of my book rest on some publishing house whom I am going to send my works.

I just hope that this gets published because, to be frank, I do not know anything regarding the process of how any book gets published there are a few publishing houses in India hopefully some house like my content and publish it as it will be a big boost for me.

When I sat down to write this book, I had no formal training for writing and I didn't take any online courses for writing. I had only 1 thing in my mind I would write a full-fledged non-fiction and eventually, I got to know that a lot of novels require it to be 50000 words and I said to myself that those are a lot of words.

I had come up with 10 chapters that I would write about so if we divide 50000 by 10 chapters then we would have 5000 words per chapter I made a small mistake while writing the first chapter as I had written only 3000 words which would mean that I was short of 2000 words.

I corrected my mistake in the second chapter by writing an extra 2000 words so now the first chapter is 3000 words followed by the second chapter which has 7000 words which would mean that my first 2 chapters totalled 10000 words. From there onwards I ensured that I got at least 5000 words for all my chapters till now.

I know that this may sound weird as all the authors around the world first imagine the content and all their chapters have different length sizes and depending on what they would like to say their chapters size varies. Some of the chapters are long whereas some of the chapters are short but I on the other hand decided to make it all equal.

I think the biggest reason why I made them all equal is because at times I was not sure if some chapters did not have the required ammo to complete the limit I would somehow add some personal experience or just expand on what I was saying because I was not sure if I would be able to complete the target I was hoping for.

Instead of having 1 large target, I kept a small target of reaching 5000 words for each chapter. Reaching 5000 words was quite simpler than keeping a target of 50000 words and you would ask me why I had kept this target of 50000 words and, to be frank, I don't know it felt like a good number to reach like it was some kind of milestone.

There have been a few moments where I had felt that I would not be able to reach those milestones but surprisingly I was able to breach I don't know how I was able to do it but I did it and I am glad that every time I felt like I was short I was able to come up with something so that I could finish my target and I am telling you all this because I want to be honest with my readers.

Right now I haven't thought about the future about what I am going to do it all depends on how my first book is going to fare, if my book does decently well and is bought by a decent number of people then yes I will probably write another book on a different topic.

If my book does not get the attention I was hoping for and it turns out to be a flop then I would take some time and think about my future as a writer and see what prospects are available for me as an aspiring writer. If there is not much I can do probably I should shift gears and change my profession and think about that profession that suits me.

The worst case scenario I can think of is that I approach different publishing houses but they refuse to publish it which will be very disappointing as I had spent a lot of time writing about this and if it happens for real then I would think that my career as a writer is pretty much over because I have more than 2 months writing this.

I cannot afford to spend another 2 to 3 months writing another fiction or nonfiction book because by that time I would have spent 5 to 6 months and I would have achieved nothing. I like being productive and I am already fuming at myself for taking 2 months to write this book.

If I plan to write another book then I would have spent 6 months pretty much doing nothing and that is kind of disastrous for me because my mind thinks very complexly and if a certain thing cannot produce a result I would have to think of alternative ways because I have limited money.

I wanted to write this book when I was working but I used to get exhausted by work that once I used to get back from work, I could barely stay awake. It was certainly not possible that I would be able to write as my work was feeling a little bit hectic and my daily routine was that I go to work come back from work have my meals spend some time on the internet and then go to sleep.

I was having multiple thoughts on whether or not I should quit to pursue a full-time writing career. I always wanted to be a writer because I loved writing but quitting your job is not that easy especially when you are not sure what the future is going to be like.

I used to think about it for several days and ultimately I made my choice I don't know whether or not this was the right choice for me but I think I am going to find out in a few months. I had a pretty good job, there was not much pressure everything was going smoothly but I felt that I could not do this job till the time I was 60.

When I closed my eyes and thought that I had to do this job till I turned 60 or till the time I retired I thought there was something wrong with what I was thinking. I do not want to retire from working multiple jobs and neither I want to retire from working only 1 job till the time I retire.

I hate the idea of working till 50 or 60 because I am a lazy person and would like to retire quite early say maybe by 40 years. Consider that I may die at the age of 70, if I retire at the age of 40 then maybe I could visit different places in another 30 years so I can die peacefully.

I would like to visit almost all the major holiday destinations and travel around the world in 30 years. 30 years may sound like a long period but if you are looking to explore the world in 30 years then I would say that 30 years is a short period.

I may not live up to 70 years I might die much sooner than I had expected so on paper I might think that I have 30 years but in reality, I might have less than 30 years. The target for me is that I have to make my plans in such a way that I am settled by the age of 40 and make sure that I have a retirement plan so that I can live the next few years travelling around the world.

Now this dream seems very unrealistic because I am 28 now and that means that I have 12 years to go till now I have not achieved anything and already 2 months of 2024 are gone so time is ticking and with each year we are losing time and we are reaching my target.

Now I am a very realistic person the target which I have set might not work but this can be a great motivator for me. I think that if a certain timer is there to constantly motivate me it could be a great thing and probably need of the hour. I may or may not achieve the goal but there is no harm in trying.

I have nothing to lose in trying to win and I know that I have put a lot of things at risk but quitting my job and pursuing a career where there is not much hope because I am well aware of the risks of being an author. I know the stats very well and sometimes those stats could be disappointing but I think that I made my choice a long time ago.

I think I am going to stick to my plan and I have planned what I am going to do in the next few years I have laid out my plans and also my backup plans quite clearly in my mind. If by chance everything goes wrong then I will have to rethink all my strategies and start from the beginning.

Anyway, I think I have laid out my plan in front of everyone, irrespective of whatever happens I just hope that I can achieve those things which I have been aiming for. I don't know what the future holds for me but currently, I would be focused on writing and if it fails then I would have to switch to digital content.

These are my plans and although I did not have to lay them out I think it was necessary for people who are reading this to know a little bit about me I have included mostly in the introduction chapter and the ending chapter and a little bit of here and there.

All the experiences that I have shared have happened in real life and they are not some fictional version of reality. I have to give this kind of disclaimer because nowadays there are people who are doing this is quite shameful that people are lying about their lives to get famous or whatever their reason is and it is a strange thing that they are resorting to these kinds of things.

I am not going to name them because there are several people who you read about every day and we cannot talk about a selected few. I do not want to target them or make them feel that I have something against them it is just that I have to explain a phenomenon so I give an example and so that I don't have problems I just talk about from the above.

I am a big fan of honest things and honesty and since I want people to feel that whatever they have read here is 100% authentic that has happened in my real life. Some of the incidents might be similar to you and some of the incidents might not seem similar to you but you feel that these incidents might have never happened in my lifetime.

It is possible while reading some of the stories you might feel like that but I can assure you that there have been a lot of incidents in my lifetime which can be deemed very strange and may seem like that it is not possible but these things have happened in my life.

Whether or not you have to believe in them is up to you because, at the end of the day, you will have to use your brain and focus on aspects which I have told you. I think if you are an adult and can make decisions on your own and if you manage to read completely and finish the book till the end then I think you can make out whether I am a genuine person or not.

Coming back to the topic I was supposed to talk about I have to say that I would be focusing on the other aspects as I will be doing the same thing because I have made up my mind so the medium for me does not matter and I still think I can do it and can do pretty good at least on 1 platform.

I have no big hopes for anything, if it works well then it is good for me and if it does not work well it is not that bad for me. Everything at this age is a learning curve for me and I think it is a great thing that I get to learn so many things. The question of whether or not I would be successful is a matter of time I think shortly it will be revealed.

I think I have made my intentions clear and I would like to focus on a lot of things but I think we are going to explore them one by one. I was hoping to run a YouTube channel and maybe a Twitter account where we would be discussing different topics affecting the LGBT community.

I would like to make it a podcast format and I know that it seems like a far-fetched idea but it is on my list. I don't know when I will start it but I think I will do it shortly because for me each project I give it some time if I feel that there is no hope for this project then I would abandon it and go to the next project.

A lot of people I know are very optimistic kind of people, they think positively all the time and they would like to see positive things in everything. They don't like the idea of negativity as negative thoughts might make you do something which is not right for you and you may regret it later.

I on the other hand am quite realistic I see both positive and negative things so in a way I am both an optimistic and pessimistic person and I like to see things in both positive and negative ways which gives me the edge over other people. This might be one of the biggest reasons why I don't face a lot of disappointment.

I am very practical in a lot of ways but in other ways, I could be an impractical person. I don't want or expect people to become like me although if you feel that something which I have written is true and you believe in some things which I have written then I would expect some things from those people.

If you support homosexuals in general or a homosexual and want to make a better life for other homosexuals around you then my only request to you is that if anyone hates us then you should not ignore them but try to engage in them. You should try to have a debate with them and make sure that you make yourself known to them.

They should understand the ideology they represent and they should understand they represent so that even they should come to know what kind of thinking they are defending because the only way to fight this is to make them realize how stupid their arguments are and how ignorant they have been their whole life.

I know that engaging like this can be tough and sometimes it can be deadly but I think we can afford to take the risk especially when we are saying that we openly support homosexuals so hopefully I will do my best to support LGBT you do your best to support them in whatever you can and maybe we can make this a better place to live for the coming generations.